Polymer
Clay Basics

Library of Congress Cataloging-in-Publication Data Available

10 9 8 7 6 5 4 3 2 1

Published by Sterling Publishing Company, Inc.
387 Park Avenue South, New York, N.Y. 10016
First published in Italy by RCS Libri S.p.A.
Under the title *Modellare con Nuova Pasta Sintetica*
© 1999 by RCS Libri S.p.A.
English translation © 2000 by Sterling Publishing Co., Inc.
Distributed in Canada by Sterling Publishing
c/o Canadian Manda Group, One Atlantic Avenue, Suite 105
Toronto, Ontario, Canada M6K 3E7
Distributed in Great Britain and Europe by Cassell PLC
Wellington House, 125 Strand, London WC2R 0BB, England
Distributed in Australia by Capricorn Link (Australia) Pty Ltd.
P.O. Box 6651, Baulkham Hills, Business Centre, NSW 2153, Australia
Printed in China

Sterling ISBN 0-8069-7136-3

Polymer Clay Basics

Monica Resta

Sterling Publishing Co., Inc.
New York

CONTENTS

INTRODUCTION

In this manual you will find all the information necessary for becoming familiar with heat hardened artistic resins. I hope it will be a spur to those who already know these materials, and have fun working with them, and a temptation to those who have never tried them. A word of warning: this technique is like a Chinese box: once you've opened one, you'll want to open them all. Heat-hardened resins exist since the 1930s and were at first used for making dolls. They became extremely popular, however, in the 1990s with the spread of the "murrhine" technique in the United States. It was Mia (my mother) who first introduced these resins into our home. She "discovered" them in a shop of Fine Arts in the middle of Corso Buenos Aires (Milan) where we lived at the time. My brother Max and I were small and we used to have great fun creating objects and toys. From 1990 onwards, several non-profit Cultural Associations have sprung up to promote the activities and properties of this paste. The most prominent, or at least the first set up, is the National Polymer Clay Guild, which is a source of information, activities and services for all the hobbyists and artists the world over. Each project presented in this manual has at the very beginning a list of the materials required. The amount of resin indicated as necessary is to be considered as being very approximate. Remember that we all cut "murrhine" slices differently, so it can happen that some of these will have to be discarded because not well cut. In many creations it is possible to put right any mistakes and forgetfulness by adding your own personal touch to the result and modifying the original model. I hope this manual will be useful to many of you for developing ideas and that it may become a bridge for establishing relations with national and international associations.

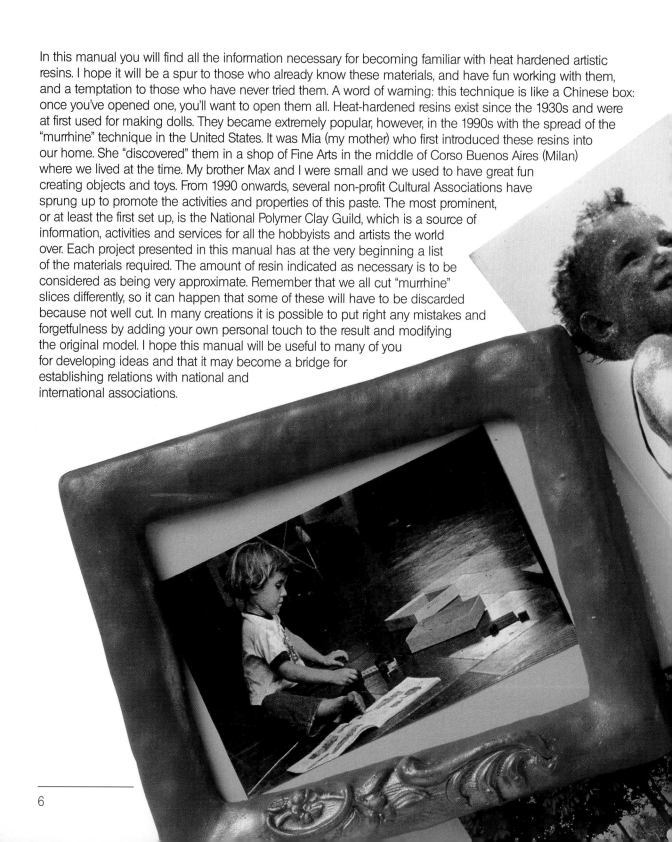

BASIC
TECHNIQUES

MATERIAL

Resin pastes are extremely versatile. They are kneaded before being hardened in an oven at low temperature (from 100 to 130°C).
They solidify only with heat and can be kneaded until baked. They last many years. Once the object has hardened, it can be filed and cut, and can be put in the oven once again for any additions you should want to make.
If the temperatures recommended are respected, this material does not release toxic gases while baking. Danger of intoxication occurs when there is combustion.

There exist different types of thermoplastic resins: Firmo, Cernit, Gemmacolor, Prèmo, Friendly Clay, Modello, Modurit, Limmo, Crealltherm, etc.
Each polymer has its own characteristics and the right one must be chosen for what is being made. Some are very soft during the kneading phase, while others are difficult to soften. The resistance, flexibility and brightness of the end result also varies. The different products can be mixed together without any problems.
These materials are all non-toxic. They are mainly made up of polyvinyl chloride powder, plasticizers,

different types of fill-in substances to give body and volume, stabilizers which preserve the product's characteristics and pigments for coloring the paste. PVC or polyvinyl chloride, i.e. plastic polymer, is the basis of these heat-hardened resins.

Polymers are made up of one or two molecules of the same compound which, in the presence of a catalyser, become united. The chemical uniting process of these molecules leading to the formation of more complex molecules is called polymerisation. Vinyl chloride (monochoride...) is the gas, the formula of which is $CH_2 CHCl$ which supplies the polyvinyl chloride (PVC) or vinyl plastic (one of the first plastic materials obtained per synthesis). The polymerisation process of the vinyl chloride is highly toxic and occurs in watertight reactors in large industries. Once put on the market, PVC powders are non-toxic.

Before obtaining a paste which can be modelled, such as our products, other non-toxic compounds must be added to the PVC.

Plasticizers give fluidity and flexibility to the compound. It is important that the resins that can be modelled have a non-toxic plasticizer, because not until it is baked does an irreversible reaction occur rendering the polymer inert.

There exists a strict norm in this regard both within the European Community and in many other countries around the world.

The stabilizer is another compound which hinders thermal deterioration (as a result of ultraviolet rays) and can have as a base calcium, bacium, or zinc, etcd. Products such as our paste use calcium and zinc based stabilizers, which are harmless elements for our organism.

Last but not least, fill-in substances are added such as calcium carbonate. Paste which is free from coloring agents is white. To color, pigments are added which must also be non-toxic. These materials are all protected by industrial patents.

TOOLS AND EXECUTION

Heat-hardened resins may be kneaded like normal plastiline, and the tools required are those which are commonly found in a home. They are non-toxic materials, but it must be remembered that they are not edible and must therefore be kept out of the reach of small children, as they tend to put anything they find into their mouths. As with all artistic products, it would be wise not to work near objects which are generally used to prepare food. Skewers, wire, a grater and tin foil will come in handy. Tinfoil can be used both to put your creations on once in the oven and to create internal structures in the creations themselves. A good imagination and deft hands are fundamental. One must not forget, however, that certain PVC objects could react when in contact with a plasticizer which, as mentioned earlier, is a compound of the paste. A plasticizer, if not baked, can react to certain PVCs. To avoid unpleasant surprises and discovering a couple of days later that our paste is stuck to another PVC-based object, it is advisable to set them apart right from the outset.

Some products are harder than others. To soften, leave the material on a heater if you are working

during the winter months. However, manipulation should be enough to soften the resin before working on it. Should the paste be particularly hard, add a drop or two of oil (the type is not important) and mix well. Those of you who have a coffee or meat grinder can mix colors and soften the paste without any effort and without dirtying your hands.

A smooth, washable top such as formica or glass is handy to work on. All sorts of impurities tend to appear on the material, make sure therefore, that your work top, tools and hands are always clean.

To spread the resin, use a rolling pin. Using a home pasta machine is an excellent idea but is not essential. It becomes essential, instead, for those of you who are constantly working with polymers.
To cut well, make sure you have a good cutter or a sharp razor blade (take care not to cut yourselves, though!). To obtain identical "murrhine" slices, mark the intervals by placing a screw on the "murrhine". The marks on the material left by the screw threads will serve as a guide for cutting.

Although it makes your hands dry, alcohol is perfect for cleaning your working top dirtied with paste. I always advise people to sprinkle their hands with some baby powder to prevent them from getting dirty. In this way, your hands and work will be cleaner. Once moulded, and you are satisfied with the result, the polymer can be put in the oven. Some resins have a brightish surface when they come out of the oven. Try polishing it to make it even more brilliant. Alcohol-based enamel is perfect for this. An even

simpler and less expensive method is to use a soft, dry cloth and wipe the object with neutral-colored shoe polish or bees wax.

The surface can be smoothed also by sprinkling the object with a notion of baby powder and delicately rubbing it with your hands before placing it in the oven. You will need a lot of patience, but the end result is rewarding.

There could still be some baby powder left on the object once baked. All you need to do is sprinkle it

with a drop or two of oil and then dry. The paste can be put in the oven on a glass tray. You will notice that the side touching the glass, once cooled, becomes shiny. The final treatment of the surface, before baking, is very important. You can give your work a rough look by dabbing it with a wide-meshed cloth. To prevent the tool you are using from getting stuck to your work top, sprinkle it with a thin layer of baby powder. Once baked, smooth the surface with very thin emery paper.

BAKING

To bake use a normal home oven at a low temperature (from 100 to 130°C). Should you not have an oven you can use exclusively for this type of work, use your kitchen one remembering, however, to place the objects in an old pot first because even though the materials used DO NOT release toxic gases, they do emanate a rather unpleasant smell. Leave to cool before lifting the object out of the pot. Make sure that the objects in the oven do not touch, because the heat tends to weld them together. The paste solidifies only when heated for over 20 minutes at a temperature which varies from 100°C to 130°C according to the various products available on the market. Never exceed 160°C because you risk burning your objects and toxic gases are produced only when combustion occurs. The objects can happily remain in the oven at a low temperature, at 120°C for example. The material bears a steady temperature for a long time, on condition that it does not exceed the temperature indicated by the manufacturer. Always follow carefully the indications printed on the packet. It is possible to mix various types of polymers, but in this case choose the medium temperature of all the ones indicated. The moment of solidification is on the whole very important because if the compounds do not fuse well together, the work, although hard, will remain fragile. The minimum time the objects should stay in the oven depends on their thickness (from 5 to 30 minutes and more). Experiment first, bearing in mind the fact that the intensity of the heat is not the same all over the oven, therefore it is essential that you find a place in the oven where baking can be carried out in a uniform manner. A word of warning: some ovens do not stay at the temperature indicated. This is why it is of the utmost importance to dry them out first. As the baking temperature must be low, wood, cardboard, metals, glass, ceramics can all be united with polymer and put in the oven. In certain cases it is even possible to introduce plastic elements in the oven: in this case it is best to use resins which solidify at 100°C. Never use the microwave oven. In these types of oven, baking occurs from the inside to the outside of the body and the object as a consequence explodes. Furthermore, keeping an eye on the temperature results more difficult than with a normal oven.

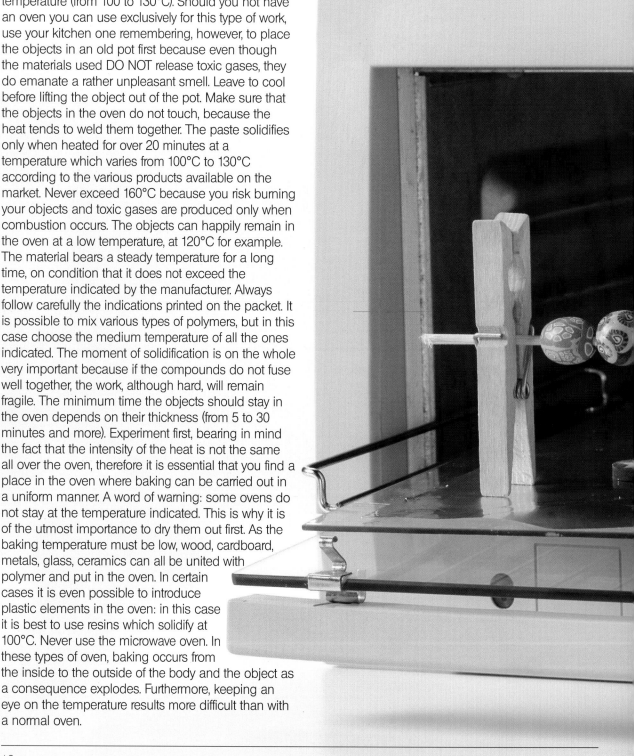

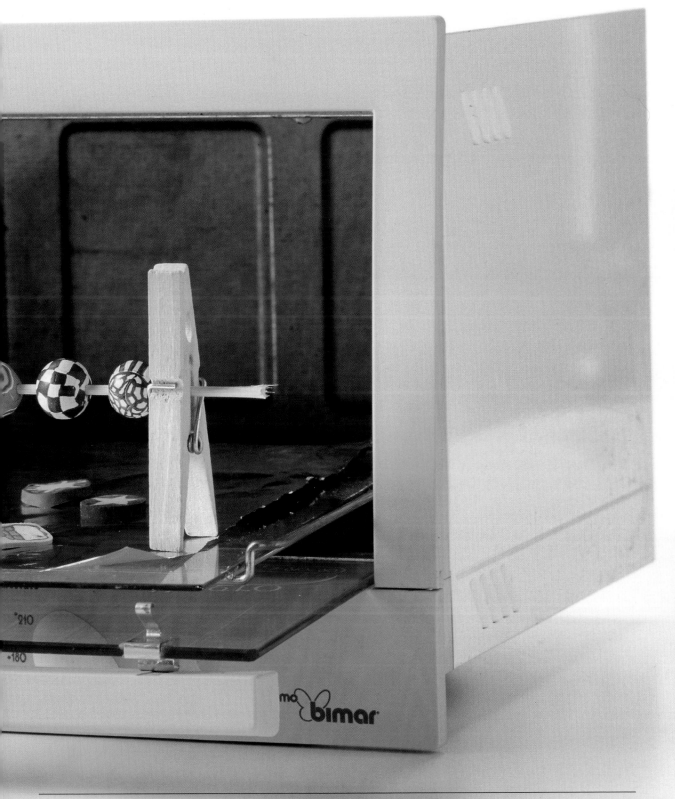

COLORS AND PIGMENTS

The material comes already colored and in a vast range of colors. It is however useful on some occasions to be able to create colors necessarily without having to purchase them.

Resin originally is white. Adding colored pigments in powder, or mixing the neutral colored paste with acrylic temperas will enable you to achieve the color you desire. Temperas can be used for this end, but must be quite pasty because polymers which can be modelled are water-repellent. Temperas, acrylics and pigments are available from Fine Arts shops.

The use of color is of the utmost importance when creating "murrhine".

With low color contrast, the shapes created appear drap and their details get lost as the pattern gradually gets smaller.

Contrast can be obtained through the use of a few tricks: using the chiaroscuro technique (value) which corresponds to a play of luminosity between adjacent areas; accosting warm and cool colors together (tonality); coupling soft and intense colors together (saturation).

Warm colors are those which on the chromatic wheel go from purple-red to yellow, while the cool ones range from yellow-green to purple. In the chromatic spectrum, the warm colors are opposite the cool ones.

Beginners are advised to use monochromatic colors (belonging to a single range) or primary colors, which, mixed together, create secondary colors.

For example, using yellow, blue and white, if you don't like the object, you can mix the resin to obtain a light green. We recommend you do not accost complementary colors, because when mixed they could produce a neutral color, the tonality of which is not always pleasing to the eye.

It is useful to know that the primary colors are:
RED – YELLOW – BLUE and that they cannot be obtained by mixing them with other colors. These colors cannot be broken down. Secondary colors, on the other hand, can be obtained by mixing two primary colors:

RED + YELLOW = ORANGE
BLUE + YELLOW = GREEN
RED + BLUE = PURPLE

BLACK and WHITE are not chromatic colors, but exist as pigments.

RED and GREEN, ORANGE and BLUE, PURPLE and YELLOW are complementary colors: they have no colors in common. As well as pigments, other elements, which do not lose their properties once merged, can be mixed in the paste with polymers. These are gold, silver, purpurin, pepper, chilli and clay powders.

To create a granite-type effect, mix white resin, purpurin and black pepper. These products are all available in Fine Arts shops, as well as in supermarkets.

MURRINE TECHNIQUE

MURRHINES

The word Murrhine comes from the Latin murrha, which was a precious mineral with which very fine vases were made in Ancient Rome.

The murrhine technique applied to resins which can be modelled is like a kaleidoscope: endless colored shapes succeed one another. This technique dates back to the Egyptians (4000 BC) and became popular with the Venetians in the 15th century. Today, in Murano (Venice) beautiful objects are still being made with this technique. The murrhine technique can also be applied to other materials, such as wax.

With this technique it is possible to create a three dimensional image by using colored, theat-hardened resins. By creating various sections, parallel to each other according to a common directrix, it is possible to achieve a series of two-dimensional images similar to each other and depicting the first shape devised. Don't worry: it's simple.

Let's take a cinnamon bun as an example; it'll help clarify things. Think of a layer of soft paste for desserts and one made of chocolate cream, and of rolling them up. The Swiss roll is then cut into slices and every "recipient's" slice will have the same curled pattern.

The same principle holds for the murrhine technique.

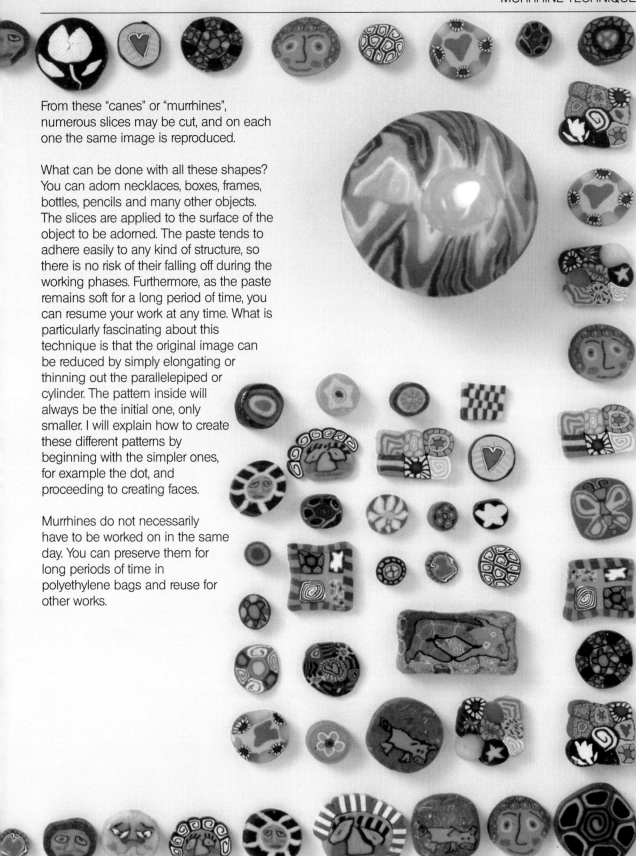

From these "canes" or "murrhines", numerous slices may be cut, and on each one the same image is reproduced.

What can be done with all these shapes? You can adorn necklaces, boxes, frames, bottles, pencils and many other objects. The slices are applied to the surface of the object to be adorned. The paste tends to adhere easily to any kind of structure, so there is no risk of their falling off during the working phases. Furthermore, as the paste remains soft for a long period of time, you can resume your work at any time. What is particularly fascinating about this technique is that the original image can be reduced by simply elongating or thinning out the parallelepiped or cylinder. The pattern inside will always be the initial one, only smaller. I will explain how to create these different patterns by beginning with the simpler ones, for example the dot, and proceeding to creating faces.

Murrhines do not necessarily have to be worked on in the same day. You can preserve them for long periods of time in polyethylene bags and reuse for other works.

MAIN SHAPES

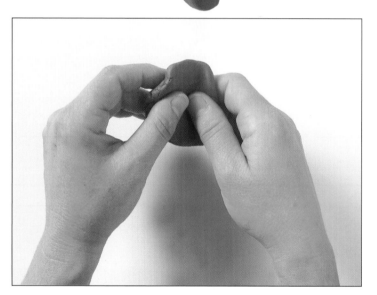

To create "millefiori" or "murrhines", you basically need to be familiar with three geometric solids. (cylinder, parallelepiped, and prism, besides sheet of paste). These will be used as "pieces" for creating the pattern. The motif will be a three dimensional puzzle.

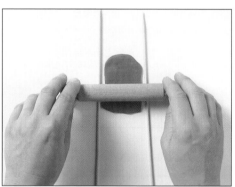

To make a sheet of paste, soften some resin, kneading it with your hands. Then spread the resin on your work top with a rolling pin. Place spit skewers on either side of the paste so that the thickness of the resin is uniform all over.

Cut the edges so as to obtain a rectangular or square sheet of paste, according to your needs.

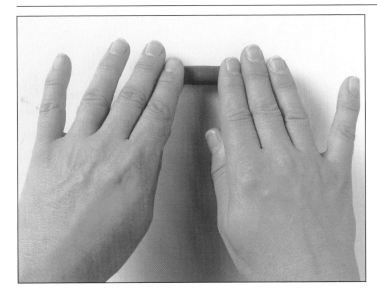

To make a cylinder, roll some resin on your work top.
Trim both ends for the shape to be regular.

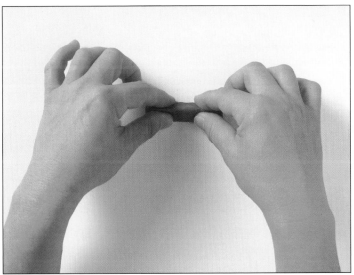

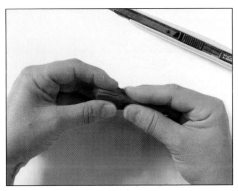

To make a prism, roll some resin into a "sausage". Press it on your work top in order to create one of the sides. Model the top with your fingers, thinning the paste along the top part, thus forming the other two sides. Cut the end to have a perfect prism.

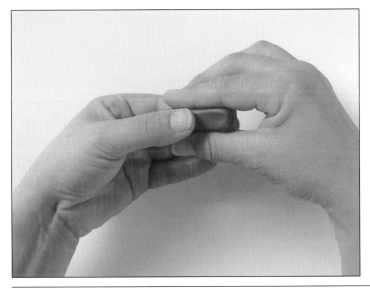

To make a parallelepiped, hold a cylinder between your index fingers and thumbs. Mould the opposite sides with each hand. Finish off the shape using your work top as support. Trim the ends and your parallelepiped is ready.

DOTS

The act of elongating and rolling mouldable paste is easy, even instinctive. Children of pre-school age fill their work with grass snakes and serpents. Perhaps for this project I'll ask you to add a touch of the cook or the housewife that's in you to wrap the infantile snake like a lasagna. But please don't eat it!

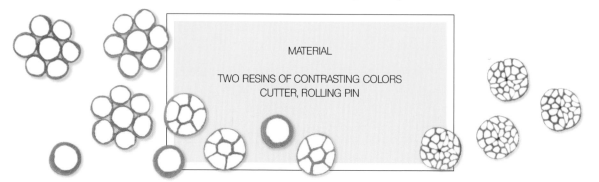

MATERIAL

TWO RESINS OF CONTRASTING COLORS
CUTTER, ROLLING PIN

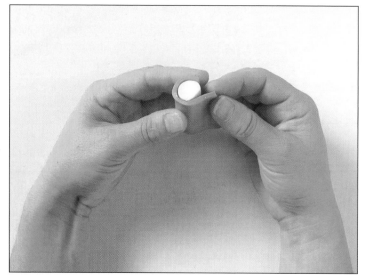

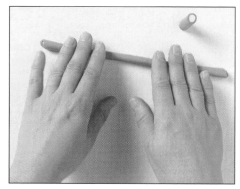

Roll the resin into a thin log. Choose a different colored resin to the one used before and roll out a sheet of paste with which to coat it. Roll this new cylinder uniformly lengthwise. Its center will serve as a dot.

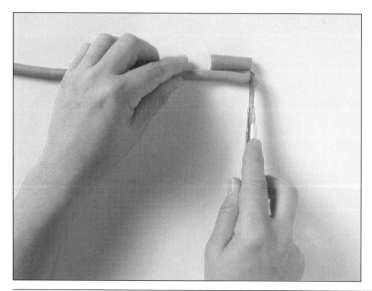

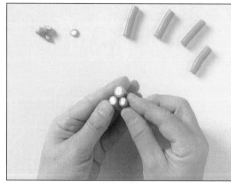

Elongate the log and then cut it up into various segments (7 different segments were cut for this project). Use one of these segments as the center of your pattern, and distribute the others round it.

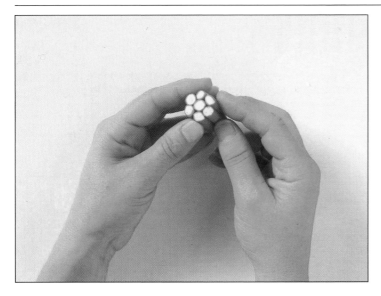

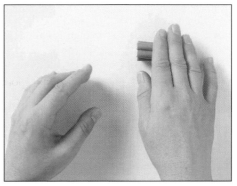

You will thus have obtained your first pattern similar to the one depicted in the photograph. This new cylinder can be rolled and streamlined.

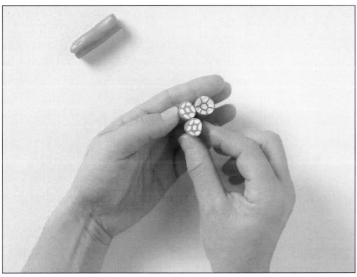

Now divide this new cane into four segments and arrange then next to each other. Unite. Having obtained a new motif (a bee's nest), you will be able to make a parallelepiped. From this shape rectangular or square laminae can be obtained with which frames, boxes, etc can be adorned.

A cylinder is the most suitable geometric shape to cover spherical surfaces like beads. With the help of a cutter, cut some thin slices. From this pattern, you will be able to obtain different shapes.

STRIPES

Murrhines can take on different geometric shapes. Regular shaped murrhines make the squeezing process easier. When making murrhines with a striped motif, a parallelepiped is the geometric shape we need. This pattern is one of the simplest to make, as all you need to do is overlay uniform layers of different colored resin.

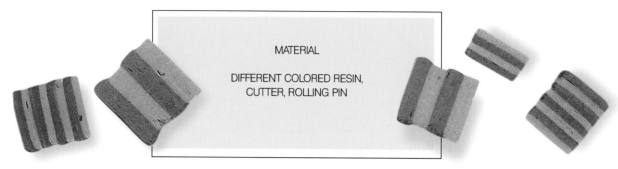

MATERIAL

DIFFERENT COLORED RESIN,
CUTTER, ROLLING PIN

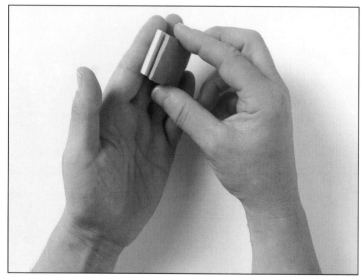

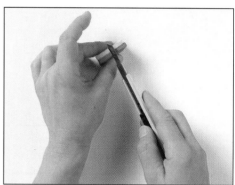

Create two sheets of paste of different colors, but equally thick, and overlap them. Cut cross-wise.

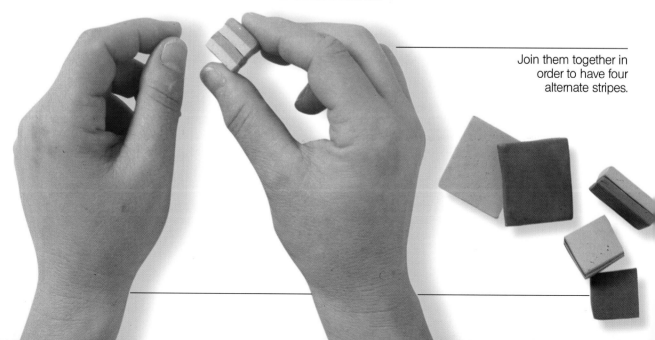

Join them together in order to have four alternate stripes.

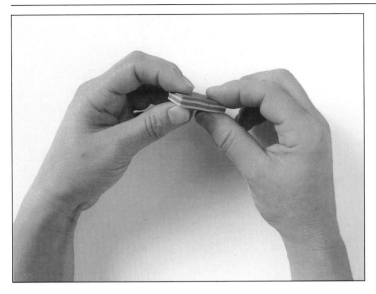

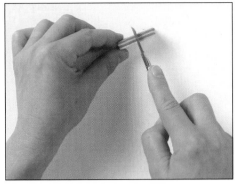

Squeeze the parallelepiped by pressing along its surface slightly. With your hands, make a squeezing and elongating movement.
Patience is required when carrying out this step.

Divide the shape into various slices with a cutter, in order to have a new series of overlapping stripes. In this way you will have obtained a parallelepiped and every single slice will be like a series of stripes, as already seen in the previous project.

CHESS SQUARES

The previous project described how to make stripes. Making squares is the next step up.
To make squares with relative ease we recommend you work with stripes about 0.4 cm thick.

MATERIAL

TWO DIFFERENT COLORED RESINS,
CUTTER, ROLLING PIN

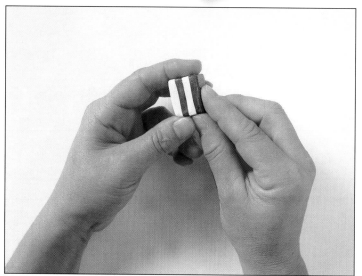

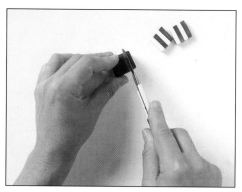

Overlap the stripes (at least four or at any rate an even number). Cut the parallelepiped into slices of the same thickness as the height of the stripe (0,4 cm).

Turn over and place the sections in an alternate manner. Begin with a dark square, then white one. Place the slices next to each other and join together. In this way you will have made a parallelepiped with the first chessboard.

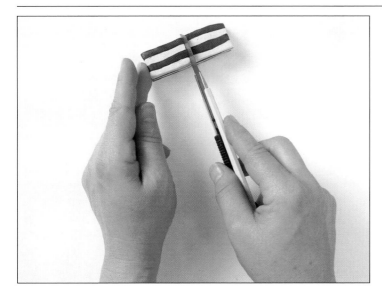

The previous chessboard can be lengthened by pressing the sides of the parallelepiped slightly. Cut in half. You will have thus obtained two smaller chessboards. Join them so that the dark squares are next to the white ones.

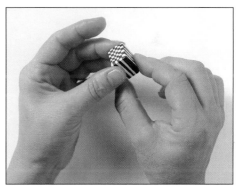

This parallelepiped can be elongated even further in order to obtain an even smaller chessboard. Remember, however, that the ends of the murrhine must always be discarded because that is where the pattern is less perfect.

A coffee cup decorated with chessboard squares.

Slices of different dimensions.

INTERWEAVING

This decoration gives excellent results. Always make sure, however, that the colors you have chosen to use contrast strongly with one another and that the darker color 'sandwiches' the lighter one. This will give the optical illusion of full fledged interweaving.

MATERIAL REQUIRED

RESINS OF TWO CONTRASTING COLORS,
CUTTER, ROLLING PIN

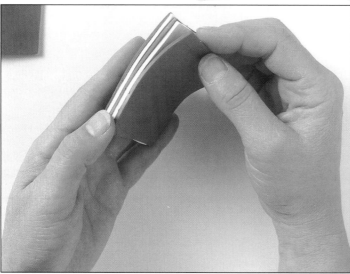

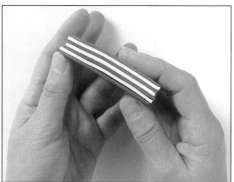

Make a parallelepiped with a stripe motif using resins of two different colors. The color of the top and bottom sheet of paste must be the same.

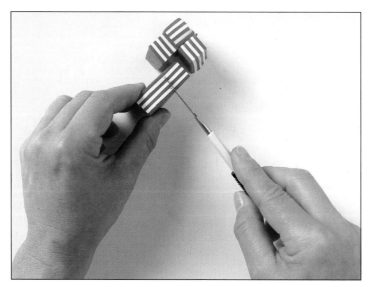

Cut the parallelepiped into four parts and arrange them alternating the vertical stripes with the horizontal ones. You will thus have completed the first step.

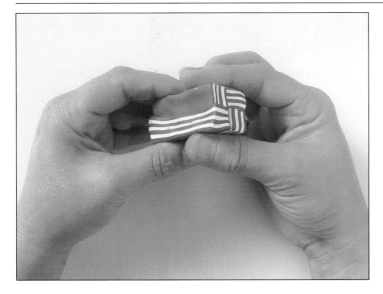

Streamline the parallelepiped by squeezing and elongating each side. Cut the shape in half. Join together, alternating the vertical stripes with the horizontal ones.

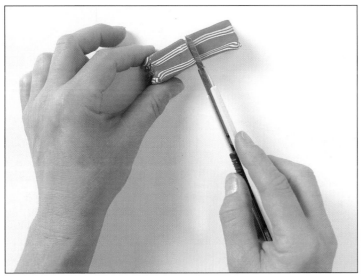

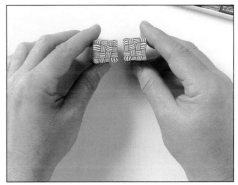

As with the previous parallelepiped, elongate with care. Cut it in half once more. In this way you will have made two identical murrhines.

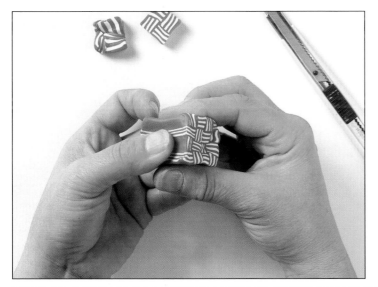

Make the horizontal stripes coincide with the vertical ones and elongate the resulting new murrhine. Divide the parallelepiped and you have an example of interweaving.

TWIRLS

How many times have you eaten a cinnamon bun? Each slice is made up of a twirl.
The cinnamon bun of this project, however, cannot be eaten, but can be used instead to make creations galore!

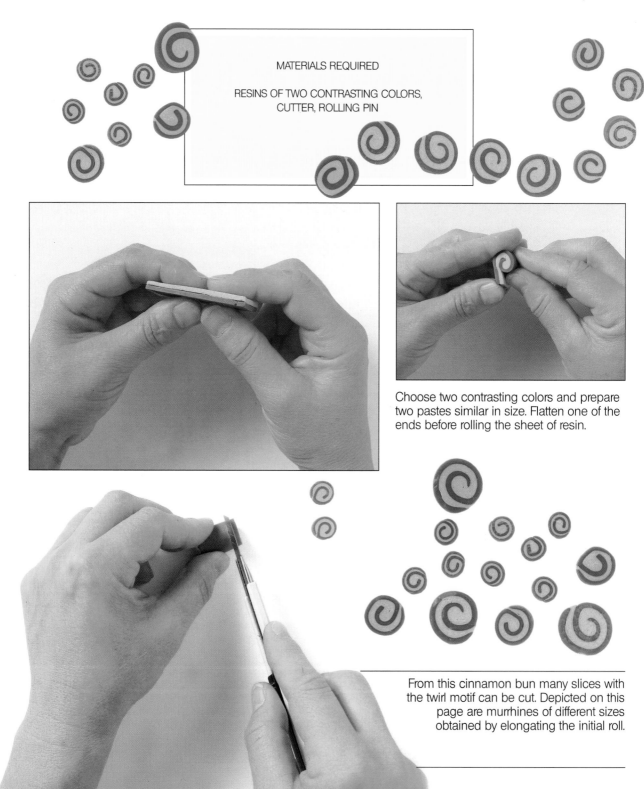

MATERIALS REQUIRED

RESINS OF TWO CONTRASTING COLORS,
CUTTER, ROLLING PIN

Choose two contrasting colors and prepare two pastes similar in size. Flatten one of the ends before rolling the sheet of resin.

From this cinnamon bun many slices with the twirl motif can be cut. Depicted on this page are murrhines of different sizes obtained by elongating the initial roll.

THE HERRING-BONE PATTERN

The herring-bone pattern, like chess squares, is a by-product of stripes.
With the herring-bone, as with many geometric shapes,
it is possible to make a myriad of other shapes.

MATERIAL REQUIRED

RESINS OF TWO CONTRASTING COLORS,
CUTTER, ROLLING PIN

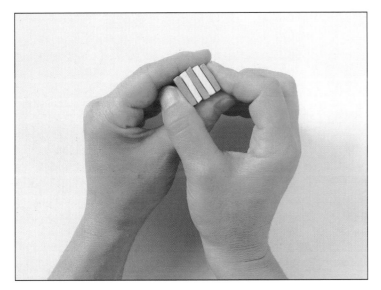

Make a series of sheets of paste of two different colors. Overlay them, alternating the colors. The same color must be on the top and on the bottom of the main body. Cut diagonally.

Rotate one of the prisms so the stripes of the two shapes coincide. Join the two prisms together and the stripes will be aligned and form a herring-bone. Slice the parallelepiped. To get smaller images of the same pattern, elongate the parallelepiped.

AN ETHNIC NECKLACE

Black and white are colors which, because of their contrast, are suitable for making motifs visible even at a distance. This necklace will be noted and appreciated. It is useful to remember that to make "murrhines", very little paste is required. The necklace in this project requires two different baking times. The first when the 21 or 22 beads making up the necklace have been made. The second, instead, when the whole necklace has been strung and a last bead needs to be baked, the purpose of which is to hide the closing knot of the necklace. Follow the instructions for making these beads and after having perforated them one at a time, pass through them a with spit skewer. Bake for about 30 minutes at 130°C.

With some black and white resin, create some murrhines with the following motifs:
Stripes: place layers of black and white resin over each other.

MATERIAL REQUIRED

FOR THE NECKLACE: WHITE RESIN (50 GR.), BLACK RESIN (50 GR.), 3,5 M WHITE TWINE, 10 CM THIN WIRE
FOR THE EARRINGS: WHITE AND BLACK RESIN (50 GR.), TWO NAILS, TWO HOOKS
FOR THE BRACELET: BLACK RESIN (15 GR.), WHITE RESIN (15 GR.), BRACELET STRUCTURE, CUTTER AND EQUIPMENT FOR BAKING

Twirl: place one sheet of black resin over a white one. Roll, making sure the black resin remains on the outside.
Interweaving: alternate parallelepipeds with a series of horizontal and vertical stripes (starting and ending with black)
Bee's nest: join a series of white rolls coated in black resin
Herring-bone: cut a parallelepiped with the stripe motif on the diagonal of its smaller side and rotate forward one of the two prisms, so as to have its opposite side turned upside

BRACELET:
Black and white interweaving can be the motif for creating a bracelet to be sported together with the necklace and earrings. The structure was bought from a trinket shop.
BLACK AND WHITE EARRINGS:
This ethnic necklace may be worn with a pair of earrings similar to those I propose for this project.

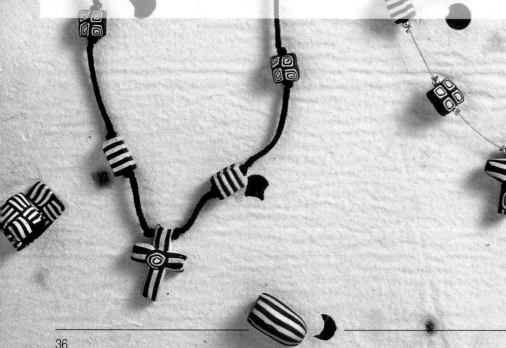

MAKING BEADS

For the central bead: cut into four the murrhine depicting the herring-bone motif (each section must be about 1,5 cm thick). Join the pieces together and create a design made up of concentric squares.

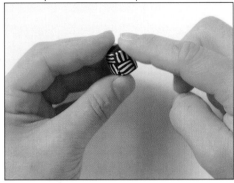

To make two beads with the interweaving pattern make a small cylinder with some black resin. Cover its perimeter with a sheet of paste taken from the murrhine with the interweaving motif. With your index finger, round the top and bottom part of the cylinder.

You will need a little patience, but in the end you will obtain a bead without deforming the chosen motif. To make two round beads with the stripe motif, follow the same instructions as for the interlacing, using stripes instead.

To make elongated beads (either straight or twisted), make four rolls and coat them with a thin layer of paste with the stripe motif. Round the ends of each cylinder thus coated with your hands.

Twirl each end of two of the four beads with the stripe motif in opposite directions in order to twist them.
To make two beads with the twirl: apply some slices with the twirl motif to a bead. Smooth the bead in the palm of your hands.

Do the same with the bee's nest. Make two black beads and four completely white ones. Once you have made 21 pearls, pass them on to a spit skewer and put in the oven. Make sure that the holes of the beads are big enough to be strung on the piece of twine you have chosen to use. Bake for about 30 minutes at about 130°.

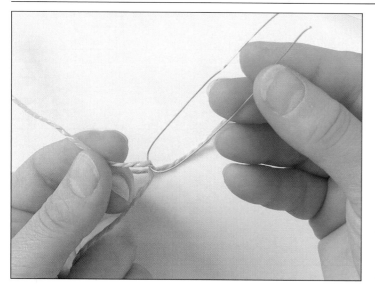

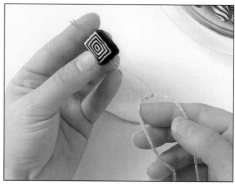

HOW TO ASSEMBLE THE NECKLACE

Take a piece of twine (about three times the length of the finished necklace) and, using a hairpin as if it were a needle, start stringing on the beads.

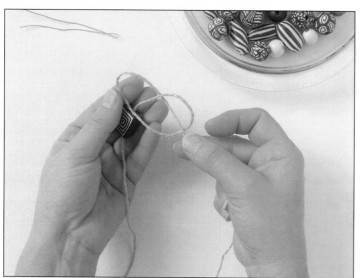

First string on the central bead depicting concentric squares. Once strung on, tie a knot on either side of the bead.

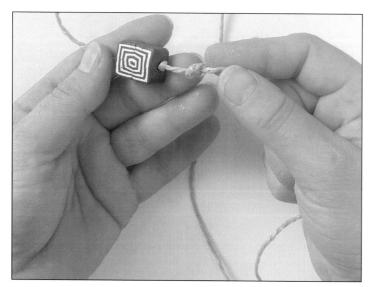

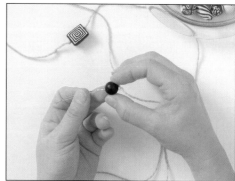

Tie another knot at a distance of about 3 cm on either side of the piece of twine. String on the black beads, one per side.

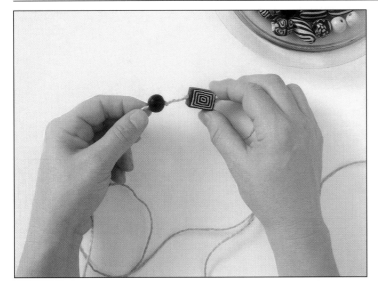

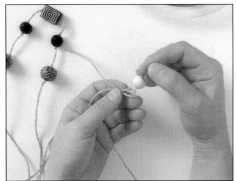

Continue to string the beads, always tying a knot before and after each one has been strung on. Once all the 21 beads are in their place, join the ends of the necklace, leaving enough space between the knot and the last beads to string on the very last one.

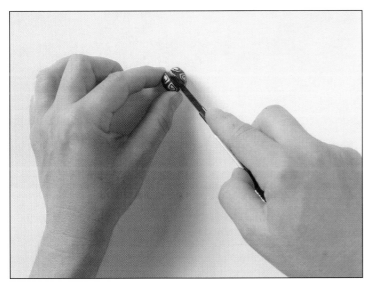

With some black resin make a bead and then coat it with some slices of resin with the twirl motif. Now make a transversal cut. Insert the last joining knot of the necklace into the bead you have just cut.

With a little pressure, close the bead so that the knot is no longer visible. Now place the necklace into the oven and bake for another 20 minutes. The twine, even if partly of a synthetic material, does not undergo alteration while in the oven.

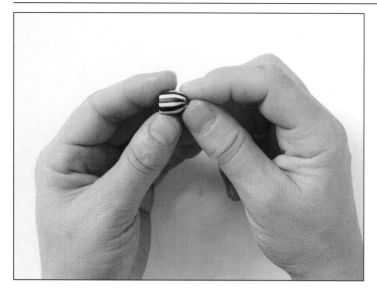

EARRINGS

Make an even cylinder with black resin. Coat it with a series of slices with the stripe motif and streamline one of its extremities giving it the shape of a drop. Twist it.

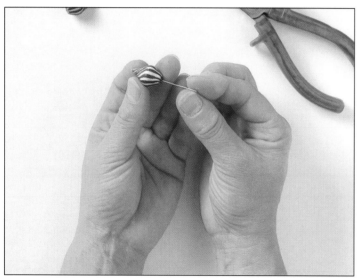

With thin nails, piece the earrings. Bake for about 30 minutes at 130°C. Once baked, pass the nails into the holes. With a pair of pliers bend the top part of the nail.

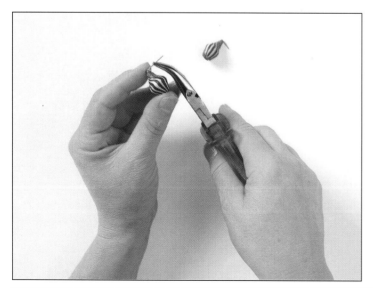

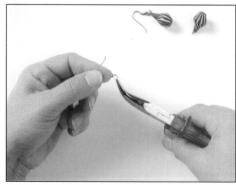

Make an eye-let by twisting the extremity of the nail. Open the eyelet of the earrings.

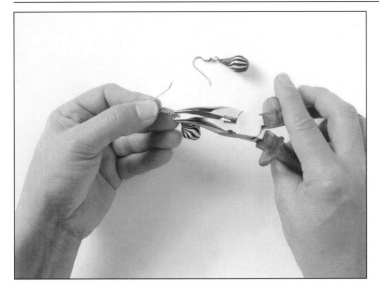

Lastly, insert the earrings and close the eyelets.

BRACELET

Apply slices of murrhine with the interlacing motif on to the base of the bracelet. Press slightly so that they adhere well between each other and the base of the bracelet. Do the same on the inside.

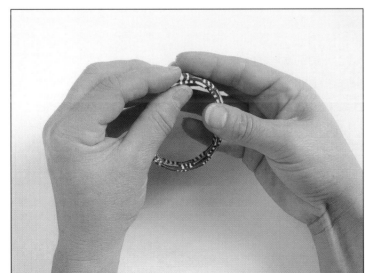

Join the side edges. Remove any excess resin, making sure that the top coating of the bracelet remains attached to the bottom part. Now place the bracelet into the oven and bake for 30 minutes at 130°.

THE SUN

The main elements for making the sun are: the cylinder and the plane. The perpendicular projection of a cylinder on a plane is the circumference (the center of the sun), while for a plane it is the stripe (the rays of the sun).

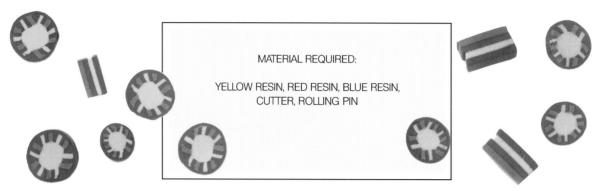

MATERIAL REQUIRED:

YELLOW RESIN, RED RESIN, BLUE RESIN, CUTTER, ROLLING PIN

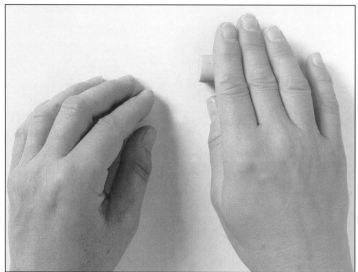

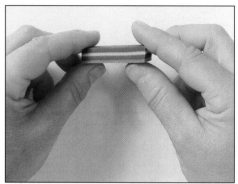

Create a yellow roll. Overlay four layers of resins of different colors: blue, yellow, blue and red.

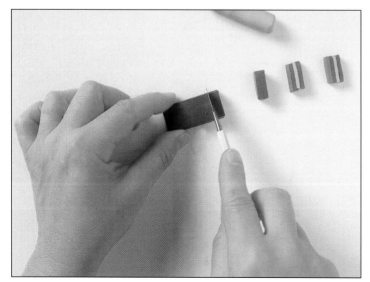

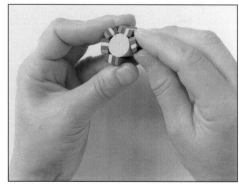

Cut the parallelepiped in such a way as to obtain various sections about 0,4 cm thick. Coat this yellow roll with the colored sections previously obtained.

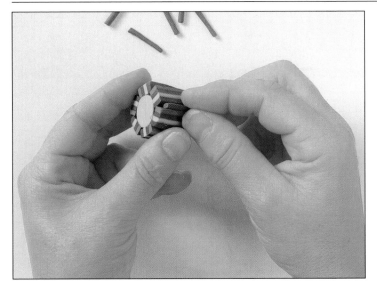

Even though while arranging the colored slices you try not to leave any empty spaces, some gaps will inevitably form around the perimeter. Fill them in by inserting small rolls of blue resin. With a layer of blue paste, coat the new cylinder.

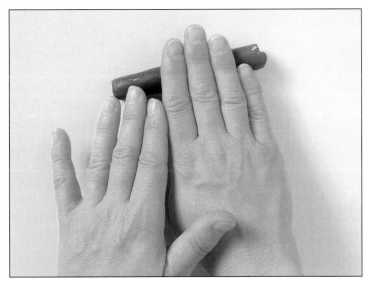

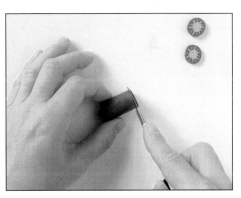

Elongate the log slowly and evenly. Remove the extremities of the murrhine (the pattern is deformed laterally) and then cut so as to have many similar images of the sun.

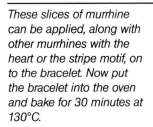

These slices of murrhine can be applied, along with other murrhines with the heart or the stripe motif, on to the bracelet. Now put the bracelet into the oven and bake for 30 minutes at 130°C.

THE HEART

The shape is projected by using cylinders, portions of cylinders, prisms and planes. To give greater contrast to the heart against the green background, coat it in light pink. After having created the motif, fill it in sideways so as to circumscribe it within a circle. In this way you will have a cylinder that can easily be reduced.

MATERIAL REQUIRED

RED RESIN, PINK RESIN,
GREEN RESIN, CUTTER

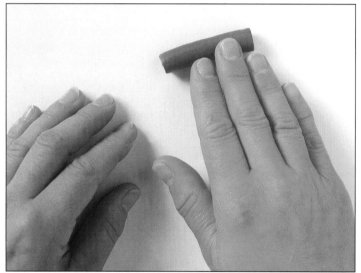

Make a cylinder using red resin. Cut in half. The two rolls thus obtained represent the top part of the heart.

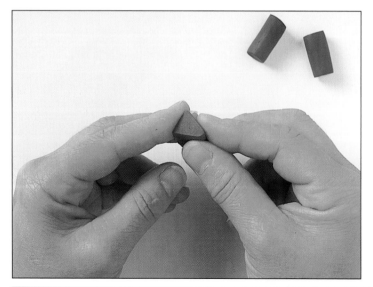

With more red resin, make a prism which will serve for the bottom part of the shape. Make a very thin roll of red resin and use it to fill in the empty spaces between the two top cylinders of the heart.

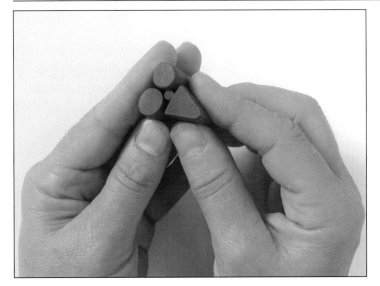

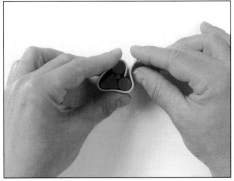

To the three "sausages" (two big and one small ones), join the prism as depicted in the photograph. Create a layer of pink resin with which to coat this first "heart".

With some green resin, make three parts of a cylinder and a small, thin cord. The cord will be used to fill in the top part of the heart, and the sections of a cylinder the sides and the top part. Join together.

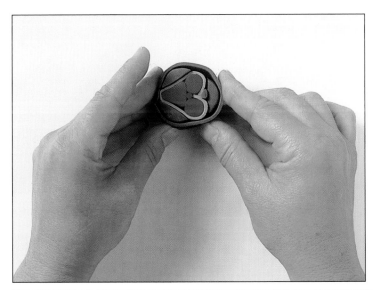

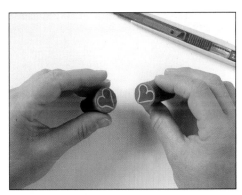

Coat with a sheet of green paste. Mould the cylinder and cut.
If you following these instructions you can create a heart shape.

STARS

Colorful stars cover an intense blue sky; whether real or not, these stars will not tire the eyes of the beholder. Small, medium and big – they can as usual be used to decorate thousands of objects. We shall use three geometrical shapes for making our design: the plane, cylinder and prism.

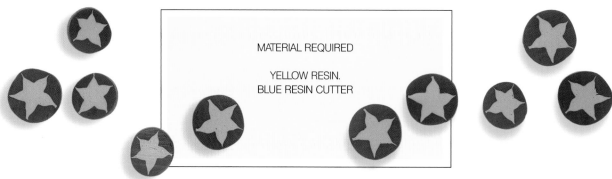

MATERIAL REQUIRED

YELLOW RESIN.
BLUE RESIN CUTTER

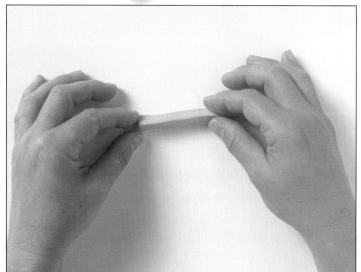

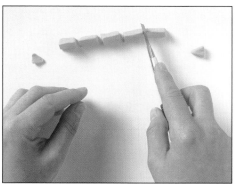

Make a long prism with some yellow resin. The section must be an isosceles triangle with the equal sides greater than the base. Divide into four equal parts.

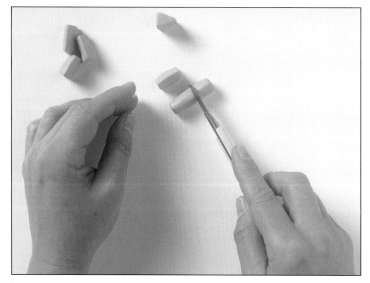

Using yellow paste, make a cylinder, of the same height as that of the five prisms. With the roll in the center and the prisms around it, join the shape together.

Make five blue isosceles prisms. This time the base must be greater than the two equal sides. The blue prisms serve to fill the space between the star tips.

Coat the whole shape with a layer of blue. Slightly squeeze the pattern with your hands, giving it a cylindrical form. Press slightly and evenly on the perimeter and elongate the cylinder.

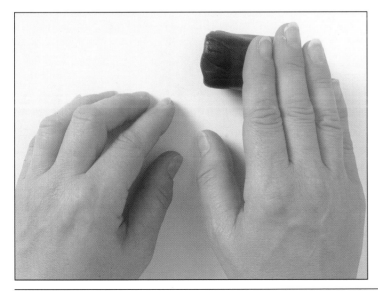

Continue with this operation, rolling the cylinder on a surface. The ends of the murrhine are to be discarded. The more you elongate the cylinder, the smaller the pattern.

FLOWERS

Flowers can have four, five or more petals. In this example, I chose to make five petals. It is possible to create flowers of different colors, always bearing in mind, however, the fact that the contrast of color is important. Remember that it is possible to obtain a good result even with very little material.

MATERIAL REQUIRED

YELLOW, LIGHT BLUE
AND BROWN RESIN, CUTTER

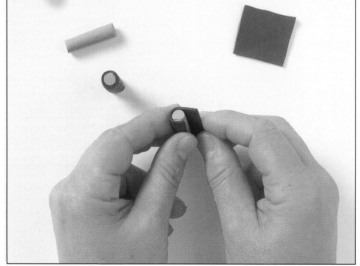

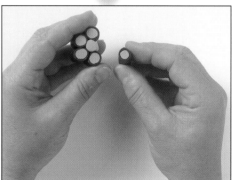

Make five cylinders with light blue resin, and coat them with brown resin. Make a yellow "sausage" and around this place the five flower petals.

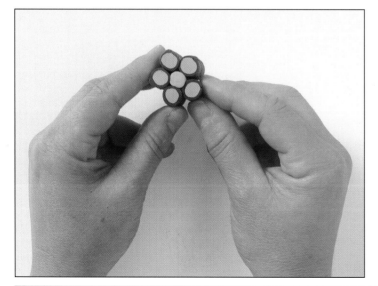

Insert a thin, brown log in between one petal and another.

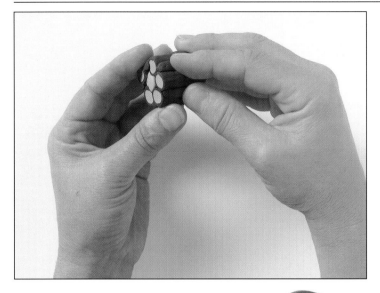

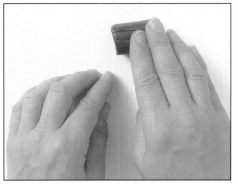

Now elongate the cylinder with your hands. Continue to elongate it by rolling the cylinder on your work top.

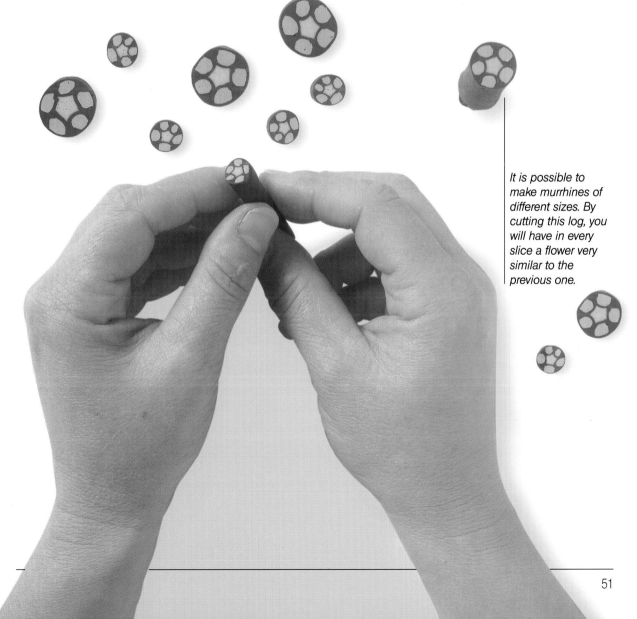

It is possible to make murrhines of different sizes. By cutting this log, you will have in every slice a flower very similar to the previous one.

COFFEE CUPS

Simple shapes such as squares and flowers are used as decorations for this project. Once completed, the objects are put in the oven. The baking time specified must be respected, otherwise the object will turn out underdone. Do not exceed the temperature indicated by the manufacturer of the material and put the objects in a pre-heated oven. If the instructions are followed, then 30 minutes in the oven are enough to obtain a good result. Cups and other types of objects can be washed in lukewarm water. Do not use a dishwasher.

MATERIAL REQUIRED

BLUE RESIN (40 GR.), WHITE RESIN (40 GR.), YELLOW RESIN (10 GR.), TWO WHITE COFFEE CUPS, TWO SAUCERS, A SUGAR BOWL, TWO COFFEE SPOONS, A MILK JUG, CUTTER, ROLLING PIN, EQUIPMENT NECESSARY FOR BAKING

The lid of the sugar bowl was adorned by applying different sorts of decorations on its surface. The milk jug was decorated in the same way as the cups: with squares 'sandwiched' in between two rows of flowers, while the handle was covered in blue with four flowers decorating both extremities. To decorate the teaspoons, follow the instructions on the chapter on decorating cutlery. The motif used to decorate the cups is made up of white squares and squares with the twirl motif.

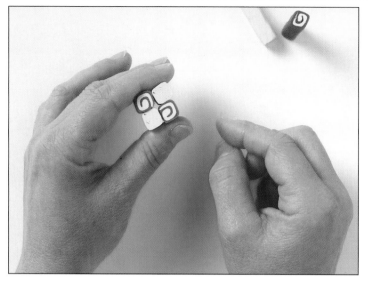

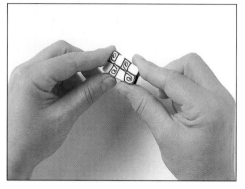

Using blue and white resin, create some murrhines with the twirl motif. Place next to them a white parallelepiped of the same dimensions. In this way you will create the module to make the squares. Join together two modules, alternating white squares with those with the twirl motif to coat the cup.

Give the remaining log the shape of a trapezoid. Squeeze a short side of the trapezoid so as to follow the curve at the base of the cup. Cut many thin slices. Apply them on to the cup so that the white squares are next to those with the twirl motif.

Lastly, create a cylinder with a flower motif. Cut the amount of slices necessary to complete the top part of the decoration. Every slice must be arranged in such a way as to form a strip overlapping the decoration.

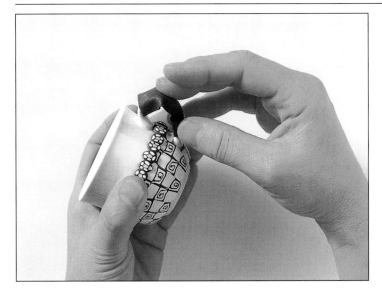

To decorate the handle, coat it with a layer of blue resin. Add three murrhines to the two extremities of the handle.

The cup is now completed and you can put it in the oven to bake. The saucer instead was decorated only around the edge. Make a thin layer of blue resin and arrange it round the saucer's rim.

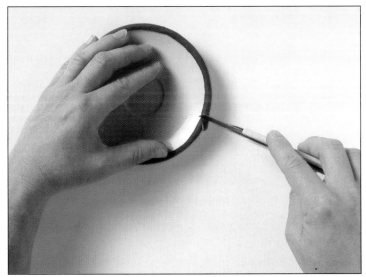

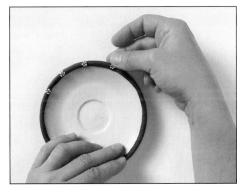

Make sure it adheres well to the surface of the saucer. With a cutter, eliminate any excess resin. Decorate the rim of the saucer with some flowers. Once decorated, place in the oven. Leave to cool in the turned off oven.

THE MOON

This project will show you how to make a smiling half moon which you can use together with the stars. To make, use prisms and cylinders.

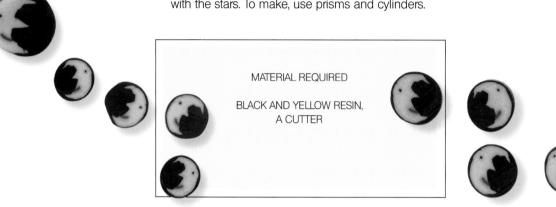

MATERIAL REQUIRED

BLACK AND YELLOW RESIN,
A CUTTER

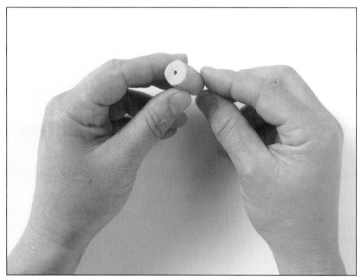

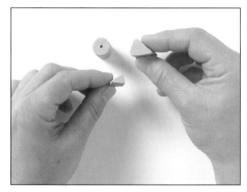

With some black resin, make a small "sausage" around which roll some light yellow resin, thus making the moon's eye. With more resin of the same color, make two isosceles prisms of different dimensions.

Make a third isosceles prism, but this time a little bigger. With a cutter, cut the prism sideways. Insert in the cut a thin strip of red.

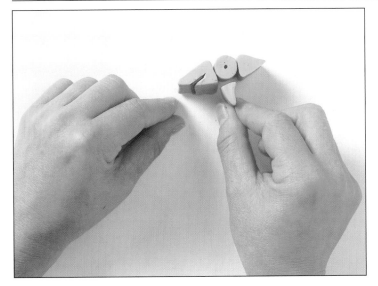

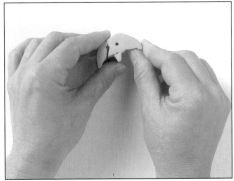

Arrange the geometric shapes thus made as in the photo. Join them together. With your hands mould the parts together, giving them the shape of a moon.

Make lots of black strips, as long as the depth of the moon. Insert as many 'sausages' as are necessary to circumscribe the moon within a cylinder. Contour the design with a layer of black resin.

Start elongating the murrhine with your hands. Continue lengthening the murrhine by rolling the cylinder on your work top. In this way you will obtain 'canes' of different diameters.

DAISIES

The technique used to make daisies is the one which is reminiscent of the images observable in a kaleidoscope. A section of a daisy is made first, which is then repeated until the motif is complete. This technique may be used to create regular shapes, starting with colors distributed randomly.

MATERIAL REQUIRED

FOUR SHEETS OF PASTE: THREE OF DIFFERENT
TONES OF YELLOW AND ONE WHITE,
A WHITE CYLINDER, A YELLOW CYLINDER,
A BROWN AND GREEN STRIP,
THREE LIGHT BEIGE CYLINDERS.

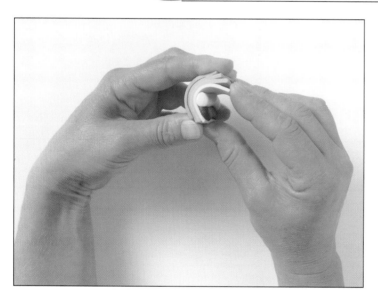

Overlap the lamina working from the darkest color to the lightest. Bend the sheets of resin into an arch-shape, leaving the darker color on the outside. Insert, inside the arch, first the white cylinder and then the brown strip. Close the arch and join the whole work.

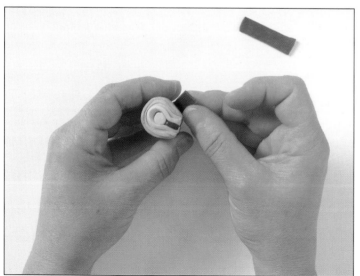

Adhere a strip of green resin on the lower sides. Streamline the top part.

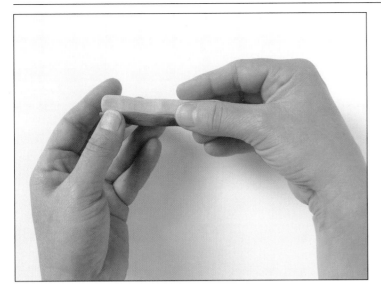

Elongate and squeeze the motif. On the top part insert, on each side, prisms made with brown resin. The shape of the pieces assembled together is that of a prism cut at the top.

Make three small cylinders with light beige resin and coat them with a brown sheet of paste. Join them together, with two cylinders acting as the base and one as the top, as depicted in the photograph. Elongate and streamline. Give the whole object the shape of a triangular prism.

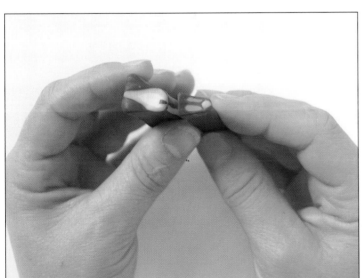

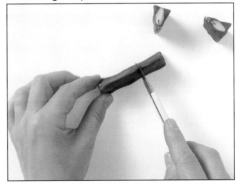

Unite it to the pattern made previously. Cut in six vertical sections.

Arrange the sections fan-like, giving them the shape of a half cylinder. In the central part insert half of a yellow cylinder.

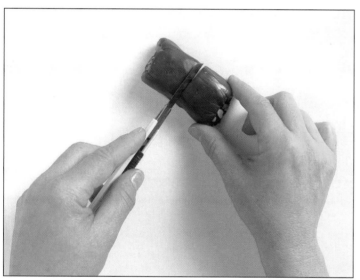

Elongate this new shape and make a cut down the center. Arrange the sections mirror-like.

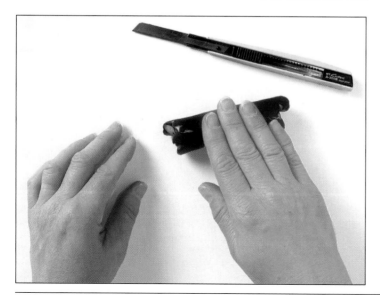

Roll and elongate. Eliminate the extremity of the cylinder until you have a complete image of the daisy. You may streamline the cylinder further, in order to have even smaller cylinders.

TULIPS

To create an image with the murrhine technique, try to break up the figure into geometrical shapes. For example, a tulip represented on a plane may be divided into a semicircle, two triangles, 2 rhombi and a line. In three dimensional perspective, these shapes become a cylinder divided in half, a triangular prism, a rhomboid parallelepiped and a plane.

MATERIAL REQUIRED

BLUE RESIN, WHITE RESIN,
A CUTTER

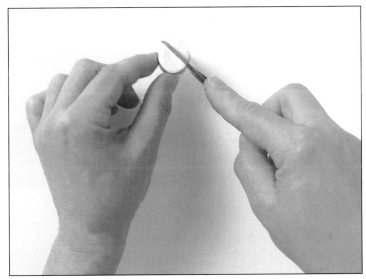

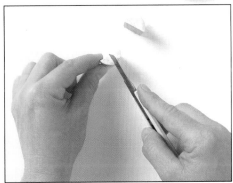

Mould a cylinder with white resin and cut it in half. Divide one of the remaining portions in two equal parts.

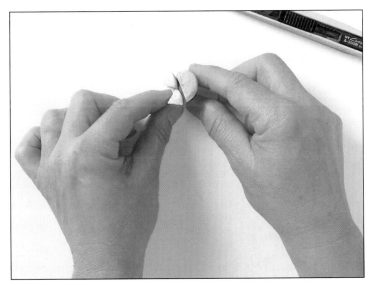

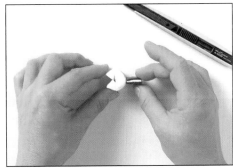

Flatten the curved side of the shapes obtained. Place the two prisms on the cutting board of the previously cut cylinder. Make the stem by inserting a layer of white paste between two of blue. The resulting parallelepiped should be placed in the middle of the flower's lower part.

Make a blue colored prism and insert it between the two white ones.
To form the flower leaves, make two white logs and cover them with a blue layer.

Give them an oval shape and position them at the two sides of the stem.
Insert small blue sticks to fill in the empty spaces between the leaves and the flower.

The flower is already becoming visible. Add some blue colored resin around the flower, giving the composition a cylindrical shape.

Coat the whole lot with a blue strip. Begin delicately thinning the 'center' with your hands.

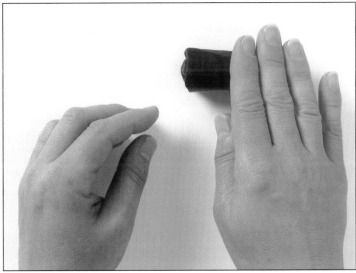

Continue lengthening by placing the murrhine on a work top and rolling with your hands.
On eliminating the two ends of the cylinder, you will find the picture of a tulip within.

This frame was created by applying the murrhines with the tulip design. A layer of blue was spread over the raw frame and thin slices of murrhines were added. The surface was then lightly pressed with a piece of wide-meshed fabric. The frame thus covered was baked in the oven at 130žC for 30 minutes.

CUTLERY

A special meeting, a party call etc for particular attention when setting the table. The cutlery chosen may be decorated with motifs in tune with the tablecloth or, why not, with the plates. The choice of design is endless: hearts, stars, moons, flowers, etc.
If the fabric you wish to match has a special color, by patiently mixing the various resin colors together you can succeed in copying it.
Your guests will certainly be struck by the originality of the motif!
Hints on preparation and use:

MATERIAL REQUIRED (FOR 5 PIECES OF CUTLERY)

METAL CUTLERY
20 GR. WHITE RESIN, 10 GR. LIGHT BLUE RESIN 60 GR.
BLUE RESIN, CUTTER, ROLLING PIN, EQUIPMENT
NECESSARY FOR BAKING

Be careful not to let air remain between the paste and the metal base of the cutlery. Baking must be exactly right, because if incomplete the object would become fragile. Do not exceed the temperature indicated by the makers of the material and insert the cutlery into the preheated oven – 20 minutes should be enough for a perfect result. Leave the objects to cool without touching them. Cutlery decorated with polymer may be washed in warm, sudsy water. Do not use the dishwasher.

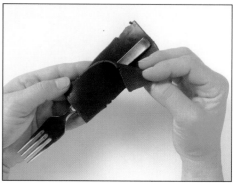

Apply a layer of blue paste to the lower part of the handle. Place another over the upper part.

Trim off excess paste with the cutter. Join the two layers laterally, pressing slightly. Create a striped murrhine, overlaying alternately white and light blue layers.

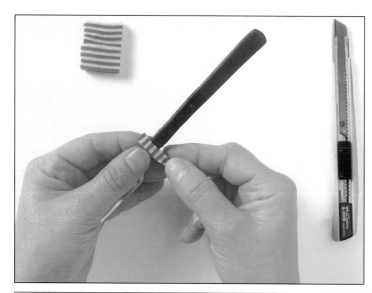

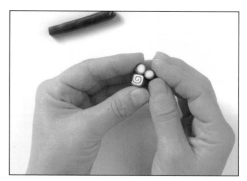

Cut a strip and apply it to the neck of the cutlery piece. Shape a murrhine with the image of a flower. The center will be a twirl, obtained by placing a blue layer over a white one, rolling them so that the blue remains on the outside. The petals are made by small white logs wrapped in blue resin.

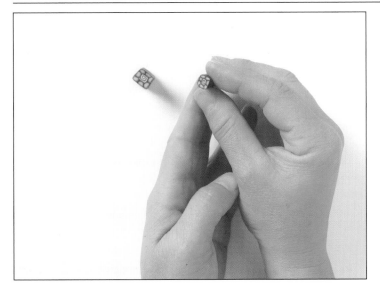

Give this new cylinder the shape of a parallelepiped, modelling the four sides. Cut into thin slices.

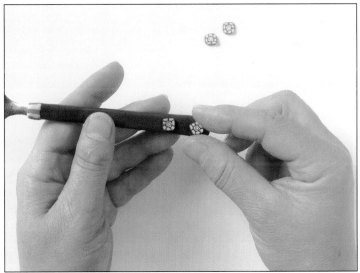

Apply the murrhines on to the top end of the piece of cutlery. Press slightly to ensure their adherence to the blue material.

With some baby powder, smooth the surface of the piece of cutlery.

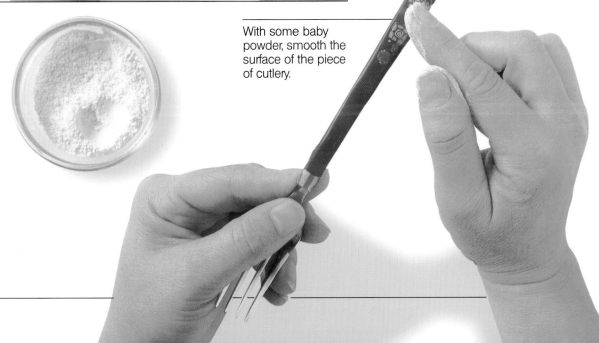

Cutlery can also be decorated with other motifs. In this project, we wanted to reproduce the plate's flower motif on the cutlery, using a murrhine depicting a four-petal flower. The petals were derived from "canes" made with three concentric circles of different dimensions in creamy white, ancient pink and brown.

FISH

We shall now concentrate on making animal shapes. The technique used is the same one used until now: a motif drawn using the main geometric shapes such as circumference, the point, rectangle, square, triangle and line. Two dimensional shapes are later transformed into three dimensional projections. The motif is recomposed by circumscribing the it within a cylinder or a parallelepiped. The first animal to draw our attention is the fish.

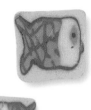

MATERIAL REQUIRED
WHITE, BLUE, LIGHT BLUE, GREEN AND RED RESIN, CUTTER, ROLLING PIN

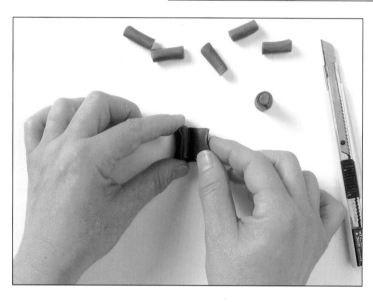

Prepare 10 green rolls coated with blue resin. Arrange the cylinders so as to create the fish's tail. The head is made by using half a white cylinder, which has a wedge, cut in the round wall, into which the eye will be inserted.

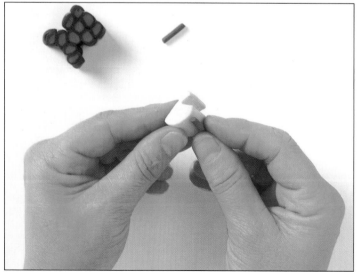

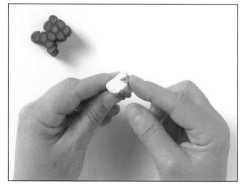

To make the mouth, insert two very thin rolls of resin. The fish's eye is no other than a small black cylinder coated in light blue resin moulded into the shape of a prism so that it may be inserted in the cut made at an earlier stage.

Mold the shape as indicated in the photograph. Insert a small blue roll between the red cylinders depicting the fish's mouth so that they do not adhere to one another while the murrhine is being elongated.

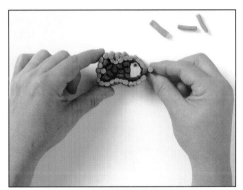

Wrap the fish's head in blue resin. Attach light blue resin sticks around the shape.

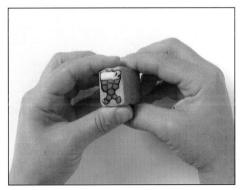

Join the motif by pressing slightly and squeezing gently. Give the object a parallelepiped shape, while constantly "reducing" the murrhine. Once you have removed the extremities, you will have obtained the form of a fish.

BUTTONS

A way of giving your own personal finishing touches to a dress is that of making the buttons yourselves. In this project we shall use a real button as the supporting structure. This choice simplifies the work somewhat because the size is already predetermined. The properties of resistance of mouldable polymers, however, make it possible to make buttons without the aid of supporting

MATERIAL REQUIRED

A MURRHINE WITH THE FISH MOTIF, A BUTTON
(IN RESIN, METAL OR WOOD),
VERY LITTLE YELLOW RESIN,
A PAIR OF SCISSORS, A TOOTHPICK

structures. In our case, a transparent, plastic button was used, available from any haberdasher's. It is not necessary to unsew the buttons every time the item of clothing in question is washed. You can wash it in lukewarm water or put them in the washing machine (on the cycle for synthetic clothes). They must never be drycleaned nor spin dried. We chose a fish, but any design of course will do.

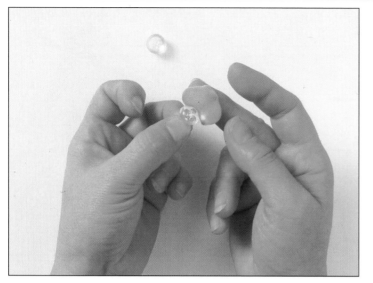

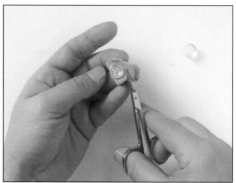

Spread a small layer of yellow paste and apply it on to the button. Cut the resin around the button with a pair of scissors, leaving a margin of 0,3 cm.

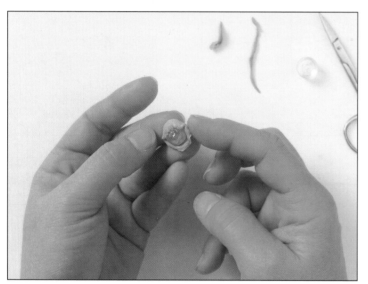

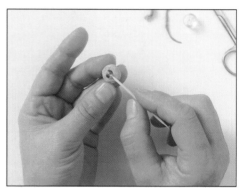

Bend the border and wrap the back part of the button. With a toothpick, free the button hole should it be clogged with resin.

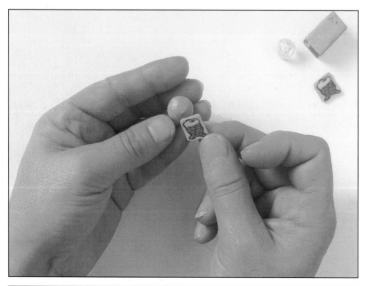

Apply a slice of murrhine on the right side of the button. Smooth the surface with some baby powder. Bake the buttons for about 20 minutes at a low temperature (130°C).

LADYBIRDS

According to many, the ladybird is a lovely animal which often acts as a lucky charm.
Ladybirds can be used to decorate buttons and a host of other objects.

MATERIAL REQUIRED

RED, GREEN, BLACK AND WHITE RESIN,
CUTTER AND ROLLING PIN

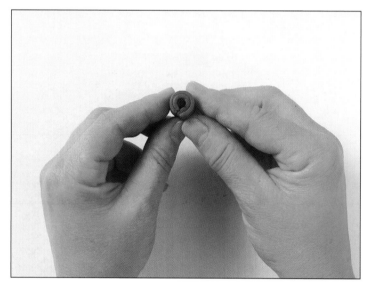

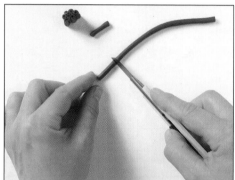

With some black resin, create a thin cord.
Wrap it with a thick layer of red resin.
Elongate the cylinder by rolling it on a flat
surface. Once you have obtained a long,
thin roll, cut it into 16 sections.

Join eight of these rolls together. Give them
a half-moon shape. Wrap them in a thin
layer of black resin. Repeat this same
operation with the remaining eight. Join
them together. You will have the "body". Now
give it a cylindrical shape.

Coat two small white rolls with a layer of black resin. These will serve as the ladybird's eyes. Join these two rolls together and place them on either side of the black partitioning line of the body, where the eyes will be placed.

On these rolls, apply two black antennae, made by alternating a black strip with a green one. Fill the spaces at the ladybird's side with strips of green resin, until the object assumes a cylindrical shape.

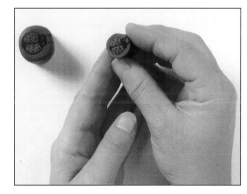

Wrap a sheet of green resin around the object. Start elongating the "cane" by pressing slightly and evenly on the perimeter of the cylinder. Continue elongating the murrhine by rolling it on a flat surface. Remove the extremities and you will see a ladybird.

SNAILS

MATERIAL REQUIRED

BEIGE AND LIGHT BLUE RESIN,
CUTTER AND ROLLING PIN.

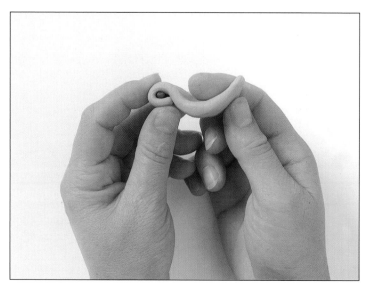

Mould a piece of beige paste and roll one of its extremities around a small brown cylinder. Coat it with a thin layer of brown resin.

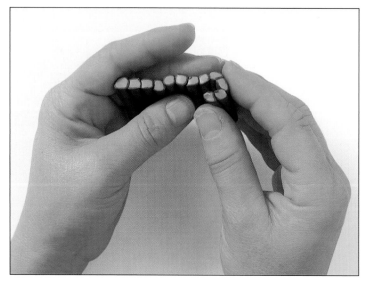

Roll over each other a series of beige rolls, each one coated with a thin layer of brown resin. In this way you will have created the snail's shell.

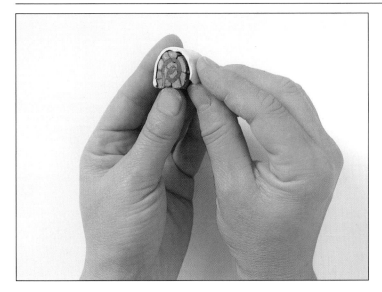

Coat it with a sheet of light blue paste. Join the various parts together and add the snail's antennae, which you will have previously made by alternating a brown strip with a light blue one.

Wrap the whole object with light blue resin, until it has assumed a cylindrical shape. Begin elongating the cylinder, pressing lightly and evenly on its perimeter. Continue to elongate the 'sausage' by rolling it on a flat surface. The sections of the murrhine can be used to cover buttons and a variety of other objects.

BUTTERFLIES

Bear in mind the fact that you must duplicate the murrhines, that is,
repeat the operation until the shape is completed.

MATERIAL REQUIRED

PURPLE, YELLOW, RED, BEIGE, BROWN RESIN,
CUTTER, ROLLING PIN

Spread a sheet of yellow paste, alternating it
with a sheet of red resin; in the middle
place a yellow cylinder. Bend the three
layers, with the cylinder in the middle, until
the extremities touch. Squeeze to give it the
shape of a drop.

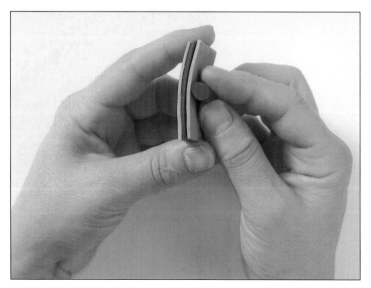

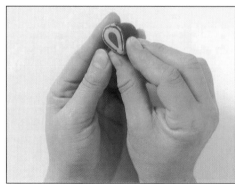

Repeat this operation, this time with two
layers of red resin and one layer of yellow:
squeeze and give it the shape of a drop too.

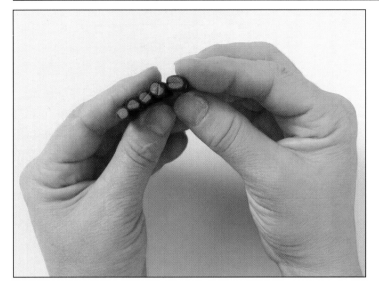

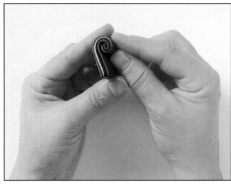

Wrap five logs of increasing size with brown resin and join together, from the smallest to the biggest. These will serve as the body and head of the butterfly. Roll four sheets of resin of different colors: purple, blue, yellow and purple, which will serve as the butterfly's antennae.

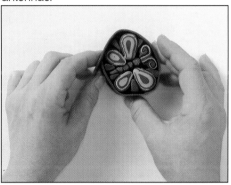

Create the shape on your work top, and start to fill in the empty spaces with 'sausages' and other geometric forms of purple colored resin, until the whole object assumes a cylindrical shape. Coat the whole lot with a strip of purple resin.

As you did for all the other shapes created until now, start to elongate the murrhine with your hands. Continue to do so by rolling the object on a flat surface. The sections of this murrhine were used to decorate the cups and teapot of the next project.

TEA SET WITH BUTTERFLIES

This tea set has been decorated with a butterfly design. Besides using a murrhine with a butterfly to create this, make a 'cane' with the twirl image by rolling two overlaying sheets, colored yellow and violet. Apply a strip of violet colored resin around the rim of the cup and insert thin murrhines with the butterfly figure between rows of decorations bearing the twirl motif. To decorate the handle, spread a layer of violet colored paste to cover it completely. Cut a series of thin murrhines with the twirl and apply them, pressing slightly. A thin strip of

MATERIAL REQUIRED

A TEA POT, 2 TEA CUPS AND SAUCERS,
100 GR. OF VIOLET COLORED RESIN,
20 GR. OF RED RESIN, 20 GR. OF YELLOW RESIN,
10 GR. OF BEIGE RESIN, 10 GR. OF BROWN RESIN,
CUTTER AND ROLLING PIN

paste is placed around the rim of the saucer and the twirl motifs added as decoration. To obtain good results, remember to avoid leaving air between the paste and the china, ceramics, glass or other material. The objects are put in a preheated oven (130°C) and left for 20 minutes. Turn off the heat and leave to cool in the oven. Baking must be exact, as if it is underdone, the object becomes fragile.
Tea sets decorated with polymers can be washed in warm, soapy water. Do not use the dishwasher.

FACES

To make faces we must conquer the complex construction of a 'cane'. The cane is rather like a puzzle.
The height of the murrhine can be 2.5 cm. When you have acquired a certain skill in lengthening and thinning murrhines, you can work with a height of 2 cm. For the first step in lengthening, the diameter of the

MATERIAL REQUIRED

BEIGE, RED, LIGHT BLUE, WHITE, BLACK AND BROWN RESIN, CUTTER, EQUIPMENT NECESSARY FOR BAKING

finished cylinder must not exceed 4 cm, otherwise it would be difficult to manipulate. For simplicity sake, we have used medium sized compositions, but the result is excellent if you work with reduced volumes. In this case there is less waste of material and the resulting figure is more precise.

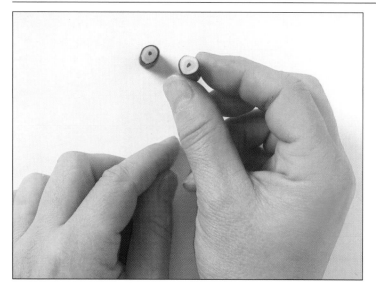

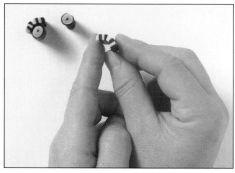

Use two small 'canes' made up of a black stick, wrapped successively in a light blue, white and thin black layer. These are the eyes. For the eyelashes use a thin portion of striped murrhine (black and white) applied so that the lines are perpendicular to the point of observation.

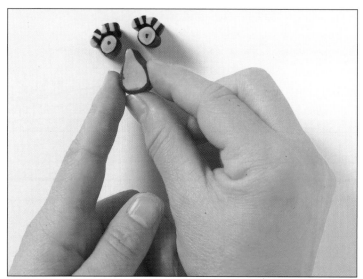

The nose is constituted by a prism, wrapped on the sides with a thin brown layer and rounded at the tops. Insert this between the two eyes. Make two red cheeks with two stubs of this color.

With a flesh colored layer, separate the area of the nose and cheeks from that of the mouth, which is colored red.
Make the chin by using another flesh colored layer.

With small paste strips, fill in the cavities between the eyes and above the cheeks. Surround the face with a last strip.

Lengthen, as you have done with all the cylindrical murrhines. As the cylinder becomes smaller, the murrhines will be many and of different sizes. Add the hair at the end, and it can be varied so as to achieve different looking figures with the same face.

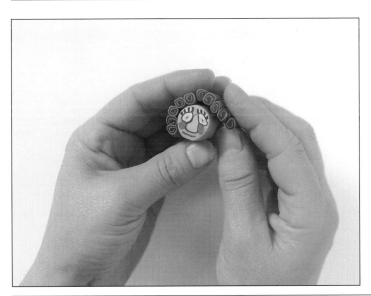

Make multi-colored ringlets by inserting murrhines with twirls. Big faces, small faces with curls, faces with spiked hair (obtained with a series of strips) or bald heads – these will all serve to decorate knobs, buttons or whatever else comes to mind.

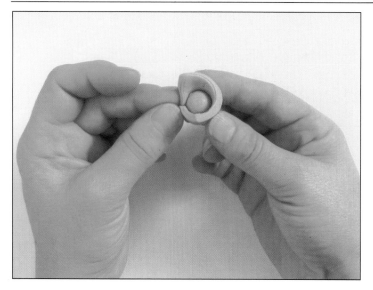

KNOBS

Spread a small layer of light beige resin and wrap it around the knob.

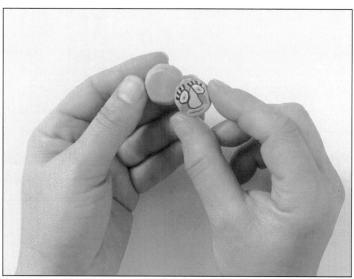

Cut a section of the murrhine with the face motif, and apply it to the knob previously coated in resin.

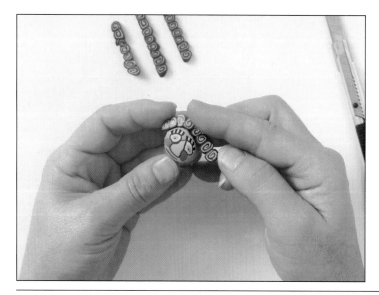

Attach a series of murrhines with the twirl or stripe motif to give the impression of hair.

DECORATED BASKETS

To decorate these wicker baskets, we used a complex murrhine, a combination of different but simple murrhines joined together. The example depicted on the following pages is the first step towards making

> MATERIAL REQUIRED
>
> WICKER BASKET, 4 MACARONI,
> WHITE TWINE (50 CM), BLUE RESIN (30 GR.)
> TO MAKE A MURRHINE WITH A HEART MOTIF:
> PINK RESIN (10 GR.), WHITE RESIN (10 GR.)
> TO MAKE MURRHINE WITH THE TWIRL MOTIF:
> TRANSPARENT RESIN (15 GR.), BLUE RESIN (15 GR.)
> EQUIPMENT NECESSARY FOR BAKING

a complex figure. You can experiment and obtain other complex murrhines by joining together the leftovers from other projects. In this way you can create amusing images similar to patchwork.

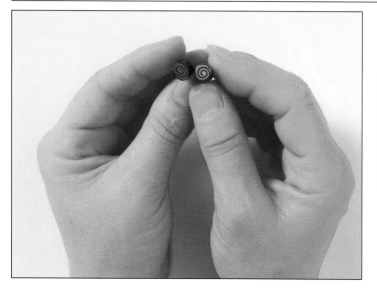

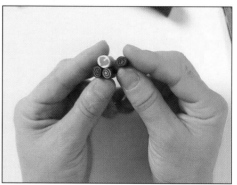

Create a 'cane' with the twirl motif and divide it into various 'sausages'.

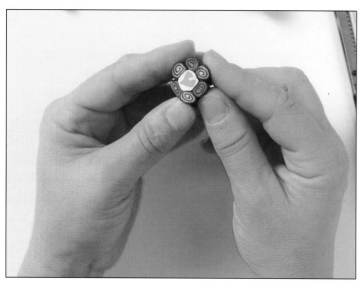

Make a murrhine with the heart motif and attach around it short logs with the twirl motif. Spread a layer of blue resin and on it place two macaroni. Wrap the paste with the blue sheet of resin.

Remove any excess resin. Trim both extremities so as to hide the paste, but leave the hole free.

Cut slices of complex murrhine and apply onto the middle of the handle. On the rim of the handle alternate decorations with the heart and twirl motifs. Put both handles in the oven and bake at 130°C for 30 minutes.

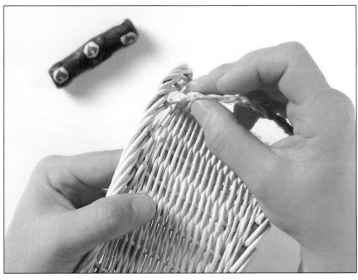

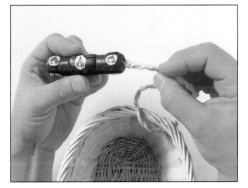

Create some space in the interlacing of the wicker basket, as you need to the string thread through it. Thread this string inside the handle and then reinsert the string between the wicker interlacing.

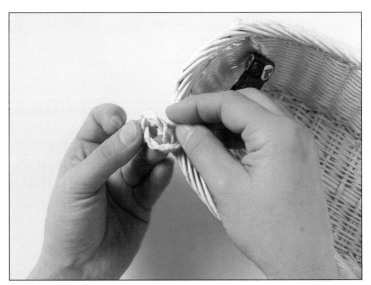

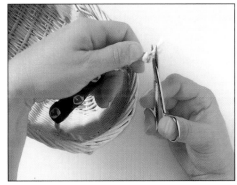

Having calculated the length desired, tie a knot at both ends of the string. Cut off any string in excess.

MIXED
TECHNIQUES

JADE

The color of Chinese jade is transparent green. If you observe this stone carefully, you will see soft white dots peppered on its surface. By following the instructions, you will be able to obtain a Chinese jade effect. It is important to use pigment free resin in order to give the object that luminosity so typical of hard stones. To imitate jade, I used yellow, light blue and white translucent resin. The dosage: 3 white, 1 light blue and 1 yellow.

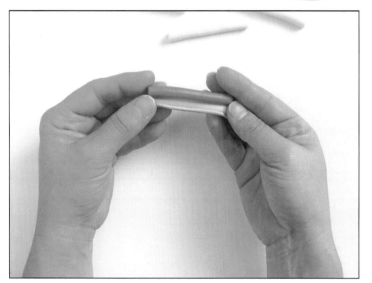

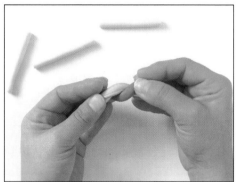

Take some yellow and light blue logs and twist them around each other, inserting between them a small white log.

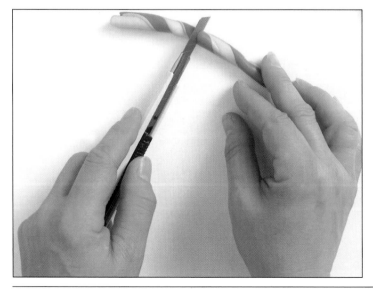

Elongate and cut into two sections. Twist the two segments together. Repeat this operation twice more. In this way you will have obtained a non-homogeneous green cylinder.

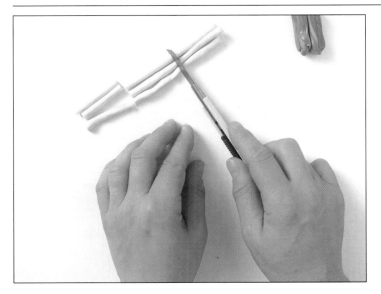

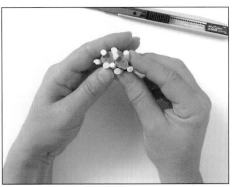

Make lots of thin logs with white resin. Distribute these logs around the green cylinder.

Twist the whole lot together. Cut in half and then join the two parts together. Elongate and twist once more.

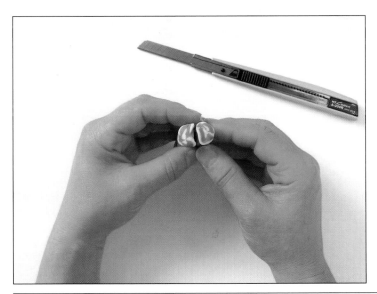

Repeat this operation many times. This is in order to obtain the jade effect, with small white dots scattered in the green background. Cut some transversal sections and then apply them on to a surface.

CORAL NECKLACE

Real coral necklaces are expensive. With very little material, you can create one very similar to a real necklace. AS is widely known, wax melts when heated.
By inserting pieces of wax pencils in the resin when baking, these melt and make holes on the polymer, colored by the

MATERIAL REQUIRED

CORAL COLORED RESIN, WAX PENCILS OF A COLOR
SIMILAR TO THE CHOSEN PASTE,
BUT OF A DARKER SHADE

pigment of the pencil. Use little wax because real corals usually present few holes on their surface.
We used these properties to create beads made of artificial coral. You can make a necklace by stringing beads on a string of the same color.

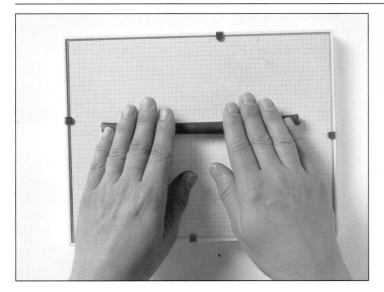

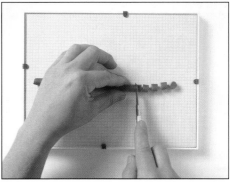

First of all, get hold of a glass surface. Place beneath it a sheet of square paper; the surface needn't be very big. Make a "sausage" and cut it up into many identical segments; if you do not have a piece of square paper handy, use a ruler as a guide.

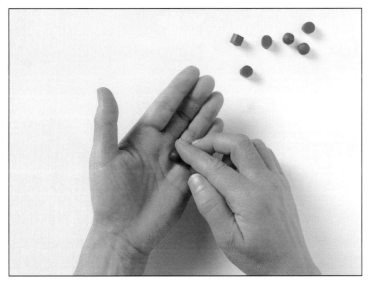

Each segment, once rolled in the palm of your hands, will become a bead. Take a wax pencil, cut the wax into many tiny pieces and roll the beads over them, so that they remain on the surface.

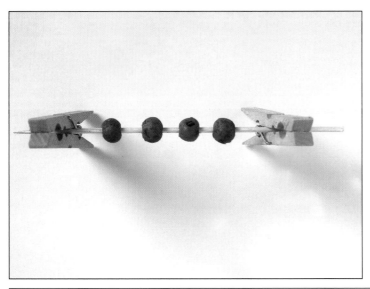

Perforate the beads with the help of a wooden skewer. Pass the beads on to the skewer and use two pegs to support it. Place in the oven and bake for 30 minutes at 130°C. Use a piece of cardboard on your work top to prevent the wax from dripping on to the surface and dirtying it. (Don't worry, cardboard never burns if baked at temperatures as low as those used to bake polymers).

MARBLING

To obtain the chromatic effect of marble, various colors must be mixed together, without, however, their being completely amalgamated. Haphazard streaks are created by streamlining rolls of various diameters and mixing them in a disorderly manner. Often small

> **MATERIAL REQUIRED**
>
> AN EGG, MARBLED RESIN, ROLLING PIN, SKEWER, PEGS, PAIR OF SCISSORS, BABY POWDER, PAPER ADHESIVE, SHOE POLISH

quantities of paste remain from other projects which can be used to spread a thin surface of multi-colored stripes.
The resulting layer is ideal for coating eggs. Working with eggs requires great delicacy, but the end result is a light, unbreakable egg.

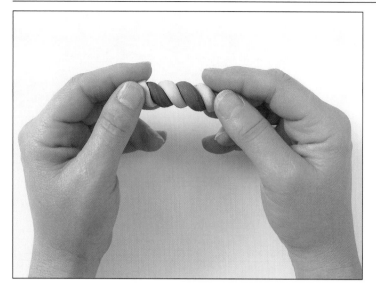

To obtain an effect of linear shapes in yellow and green, form two cylinders of yellow and light blue resin respectively, and twist them around each other. Roll out and spread the cylinder on your work top.

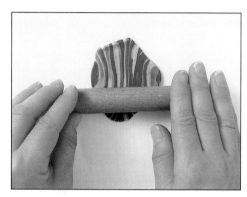

Roll over the paste thus obtained and twirl it round again. Flatten it once more and lengthen the layer with a rolling pin. Roll over the new layer once more.

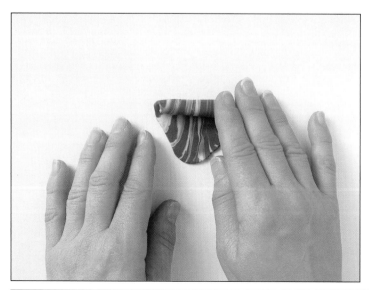

Roll once again, flatten and spread as in the previous steps. The blue will have amalgamated with the yellow in certain points, creating a green grain, but there will also be strips of a more yellow color.

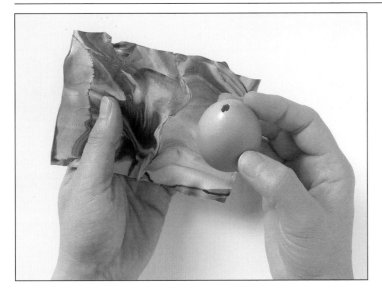

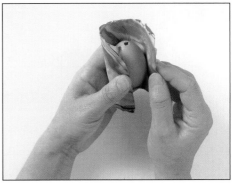

Having emptied the egg, rinsed and dried it, wrap it in a layer of marbled paste.

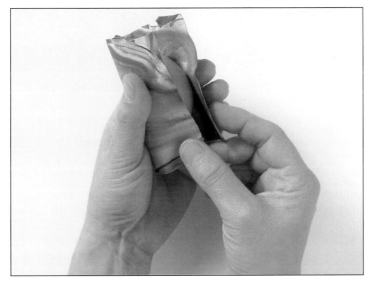

Press the resin on to the surface of the egg and on to its two extremities, leaving free three folds, similar to wings.

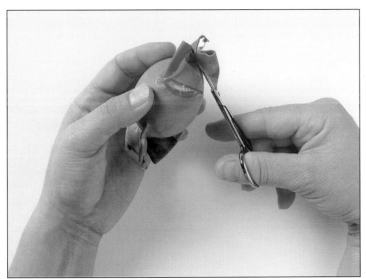

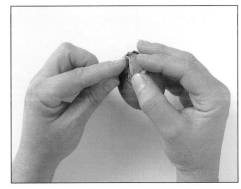

Cut these wings with a scissors; with your index finger, unite any surface points which have remained open after cutting.

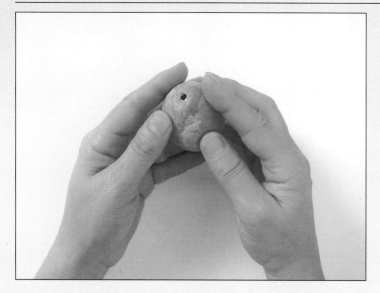

Lasciate scoperti i fori nei poli.
Con del talco, lisciate la superficie
e prestate attenzione affinché la resina
aderisca bene all'uovo e non ci siano bolle
d'aria.

Pass a skewer through the holes and use
pegs as supports during baking. Bake for
30 minutes in an oven at 130°C.

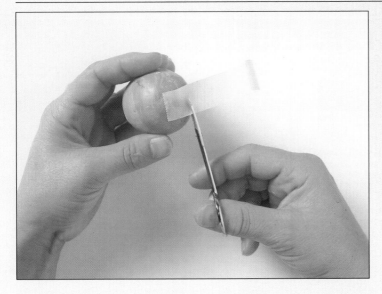

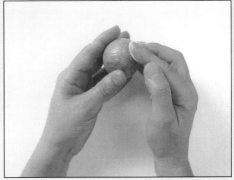

When the egg has cooled, cover the two folds with a piece of paper adhesive tape in order to be able to position a thin layer of paste without it falling inside.

Cover the adhesive tape with resin and smooth with some baby powder. Place the egg once more in the oven on a smooth surface. After about 15 minutes take it out and let it cool. Polish the surface with a polishing sponge.

DABBED SURFACES

Rough surfaces do not only give a particular sensation when touched, but they also reflect light differently. Besides, they also offer a means to hide small defects in our material. To impress a grain on material is an easy procedure, which may also be applied to limited parts of the work. One of the most frequent problems to occur when a surface is being covered is the presence of areas with more material than others, or the appearance of small air bubbles after baking. Even if these defects are minimum, they can be noticed at first glance. Using a dab and transforming a smooth surface into a rough one is the best way to avoid such defects.

A BATHROOM SET

Rose and light blue are very suitable for a bathroom. Because resin is waterproof and has high resistance,

> MATERIAL REQUIRED
>
> A COMB, A BRUSH, THE BODY OF ANOTHER BRUSH, AN OVAL MIRROR CUT TO SIZE, PINK RESIN (100 GR.), LIGHT BLUE RESIN (30 GR.), ROLLING PIN, CUTTER, GLUE TO ATTACH THE MIRROR AND A DAB

objects created with it can be washed. The brush and the structure for the mirror were bought at the local market, but are to be found in many shops. They are made in wood. The mirror has as its base the body of a brush. The glass was cut to measure. The comb is in plastic and must therefore be baked without exceeding the temperature of 100/110° C (a polymer was used and baking at 100°C is advised). Leave to cool in the oven.

It may seem strange that plastic objects can be put in the oven, but many types bear the heat. Some products soften, but it is enough to leave them cool within the oven to avoid any deformity. Our material is also PVC, I would suggest, however, a trial run by placing the object in the oven without decoration for about 10 minutes at 100-110°C.

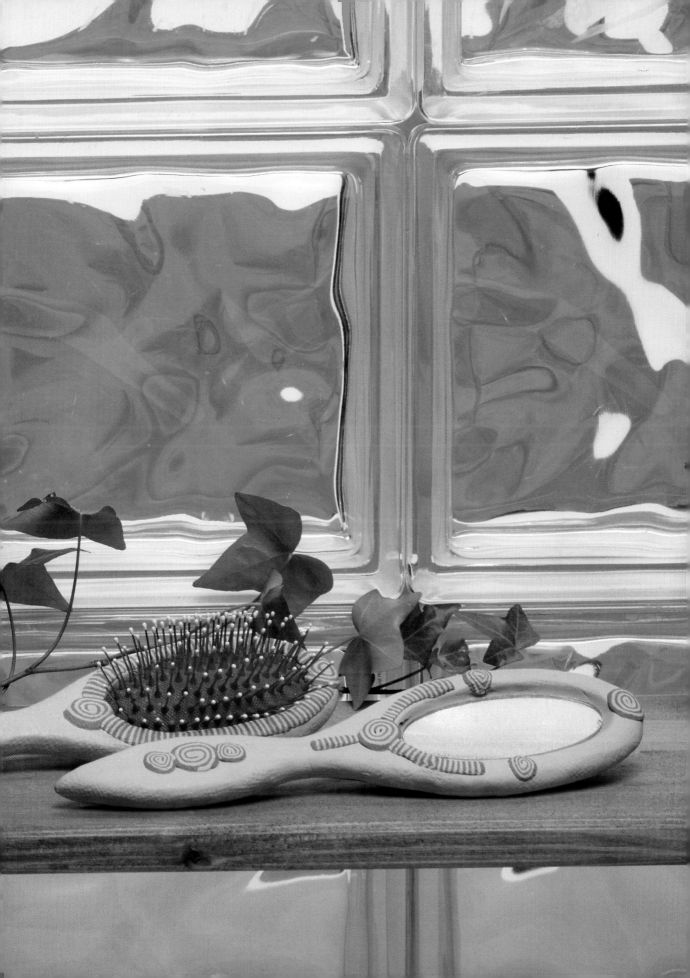

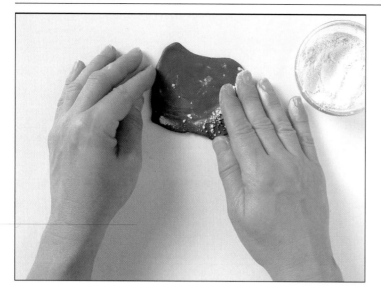

Cover the surface with baby powder. Place a wide-meshed piece of cloth over the paste and pass the rolling pin over it. Press so as to leave the mark of the fabric on the surface.

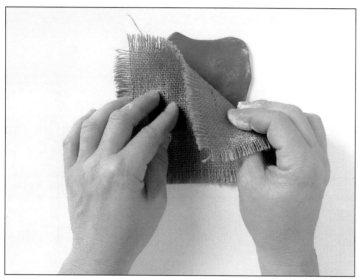

Remove the fabric, which will come away easily from the resin thanks to the baby powder sprinkled previously. You can now see the grain of the fabric reproduced on the surface.

If the object you are working is not flat as in the previous example, it is advisable to make a dab. Make a small ball with tinfoil and cover it with a piece of wide-meshed fabric. With this dab, you can happily work on curved surfaces.

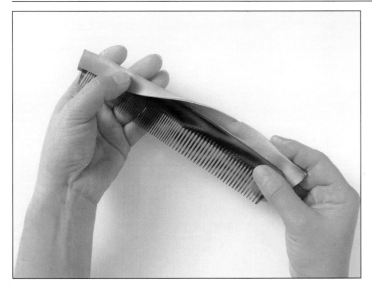

Prepare a sheet of paste with which to wrap the top part of the comb. Give the paste the shape of the comb. Cut any excess paste at the two extremities with a cutter.

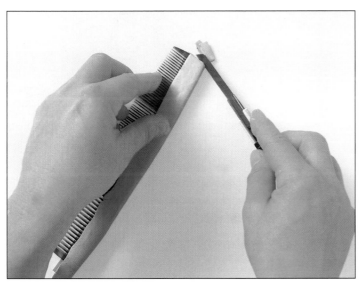

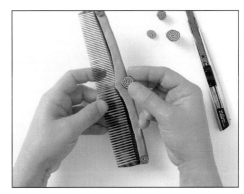

Remove any excess resin and trim the edges. Apply the murrhines starting with the twirl motif at the center of the comb.

Continue to decorate with murrhines with the stripe motif. Dab the surface.

Remove the inner part of the brush. Spread a thin layer of pink resin and cut out the shape of the brush, leaving a margin of 0,5 cm. Repeat this operation for the top part. Cut the inside oval, leaving a margin.

With a toothpick, tuck in the internal rim. Apply the resin to the bottom part of the brush's body and unite the borders.

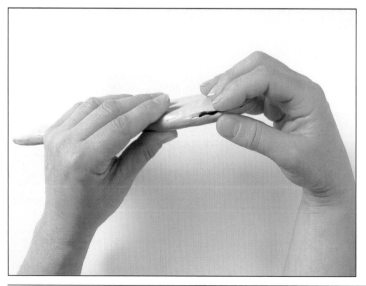

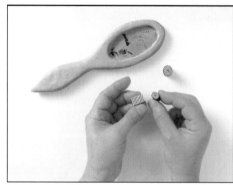

Create a murrhine with a stripe motif, overlaying alternately pink and blue resin and one with the twirl motif, rolling two overlaying sheets of paste made with the same colors used previously.

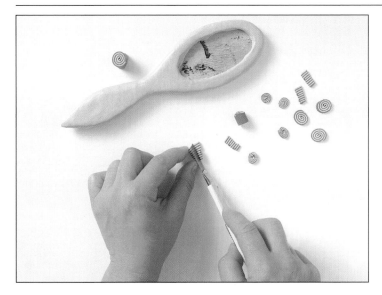

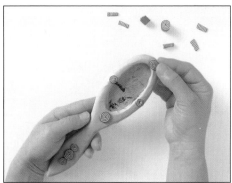

After having cut the slices, apply them to the base, pressing quite strongly for them to adhere well on the surface.

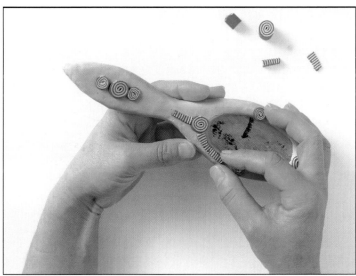

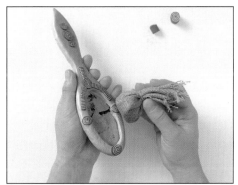

Continue the operation until you have completed the decoration. Dab the whole surface with a tampon made with wide-meshed material. Now bake in the oven for 30 minutes at 130°C. Leave to cool.

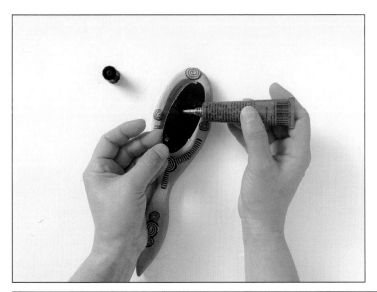

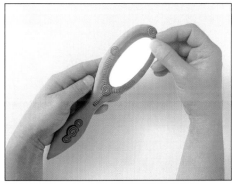

Apply the glue and insert the mirror. For the brush, follow the same instructions for the mirror (when you tuck in the borders, leave enough space to reinsert the sponge with the bristles, once its base is baked).

PURPURIN

CHRISTMAS FESTOONS
As I have already mentioned, it is important to have a clean work surface because all types of dust and grit remains attached to plastic. Exploiting this characteristic to the utmost, not always negative, we made Christmas balls, coating them with purpurin. This brilliant powder is easily incorporated into the resin. The surface then

MATERIAL REQUIRED

20 GR. BLUE RESIN, 5 GR. WHITE RESIN, STAR-SHAPED MOULD, THIN WIRE, PLIERS, CUTTER, TINFOIL AND PURPURIN.

assumes a "shiny" aspect, suitable for Christmas decorations. Available on the market are yellow, red, white, green, etc purpurin. Always bear in mind the fact that the color of the finished object does not only depend on the color of the chosen resin, but also by the powder used. Use these small particles carefully to avoid finding them scattered all over the house.

Crumple some tinfoil, giving it a spherical shape. The balls thus obtained must not be too compact, otherwise inserting the hook, used for hanging purposes, may present some difficulties.

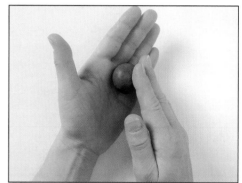

Spread a sheet of paste in which you will wrap the ball. Smooth it in the palm of your hands.

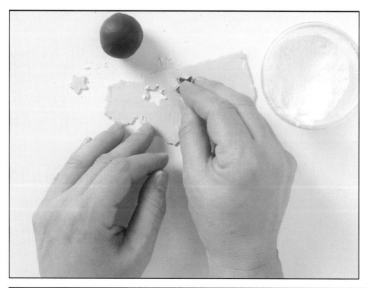

Flatten some white resin and, with a star-shaped mould, cut out a sufficient amount of stars to apply on the ball. Press slightly for them to adhere well to the surface.

Dip your finger into the purpurin and distribute it on the surface of the ball.

Perforate the ball with a skewer and, with the aid of a pair of pliers, insert a piece of thin wire. Mould it into the shape of a button-hole. Trim the hole that you have just made. Put the ball into the oven at 130°C and bake for approximately 30 minutes.

WITH GOLD LAMINA

Metal lamina, available from Fine Arts shops and some hardware shops, have always been used to decorate different types of material.
They come in very thin sheets of paste in the following colors: gold, silver, copper, etc...
They must be manipulated very carefully because a slight movement of air can move them.

MATERIAL REQUIRED

A METAL REFILL CARTRIDGE FOR BIROS, ABOUT 30 GR.
BLUE MOULDABLE PASTE, A GOLD LAMINA, 10 GR.
LEFTOVER RESIN, A CARD, PASTA MACHINE OR ROLLING
PIN, EQUIPMENT NECESSARY FOR BAKING.

Resin coated in material can be used to make an endless variety of projects.
In this project, the pen was decorated first, while the base on which to rest it was made at a second stage.
The objects, once completed, are baked at a low temperature (110/110°) for 20 minutes.

On a thin sheet of resin, place a piece of gold lamina. Press slightly to unite the two surfaces. If you have a pasta machine handy, used exclusively for working polymers, register it at the greatest thickness and pass the two strips through. The result will be a "fragmented" gold motif. You can spread the paste with a rolling pin. In this case exercise a slight, uniform pressure over the whole surface in order to obtain regular "fragmentation".

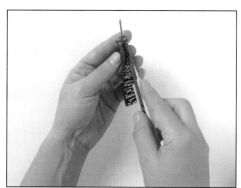

Wrap the pen's refill with the strip just obtained, leaving the area around the tip free. Remove any excess resin.

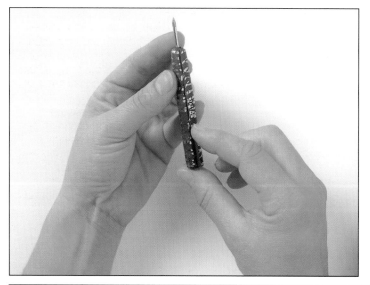

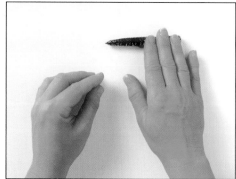

You have now obtained a three quarters covered pen. Roll the pen until the resin coats the whole surface of the refill. Make sure the lower end is thinner.

Remove any excess paste. Turn the tip round.

Round the top end of the pen. Apply the same gold motif on to a ball made from leftovers. This will serve as the pen's supporting structure.

The work being completed, it is now time to bake. You are probably asking yourselves whether the cartridge of the fountain pen won't get ruined in the oven. The answer is that nothing will happen if the temperature doesn't exceed 110°C and if the object is placed in a cold oven.
Fold a Bristol type piece of cardboard concertina-style and place the pen on one of the folds before putting it in the oven. Thus protected, polymer will not be deformed during baking.
Bake the pen for 20 minutes. Should the temperature be higher than that indicated, you risk having a pen that doesn't write once removed from the oven. And that would be a great shame!

REPRODUCING AN IMAGE

Another effect you can obtain using polymers is that given by transposing an image on paper. The image, once "transposed" on the pasta, will be reproduced mirror-like.

The images created with chalk are those which 'adhere' best to polymers. Chalk powder is united to resin and, after baking, the color becomes permanent.

Take your chosen stencil and place it on a sheet of drawing paper. Draw the shape with colored chalk so that its surface is well covered.

Prepare a sheet of resin that can hold the image.

Turn the picture on to the material, pressing the whole surface slightly. The picture will thus be impressed on the paste. Put in the oven for 15 minutes at 130°C.

Once cooled, spread some glue on the back of the paste and attach it to the album.

THE IMPRINT TECHNIQUE

Synthetic paste can reproduce particulars down to the slightest details. Thanks to this characteristic, it can be used to make a mould faithful to the original model. The mould technique has endless applications. A cameo, a coin may duplicated, as well as part of a wide surface. You can create a motif and then obtain endless copies of it through the technique illustrated in the following pages. Should you want to devise the object yourselves, you must first design and make it with the paste and, when completed, put it in the oven at the temperature indicated. After baking, leave to cool and make the imprint the same way in which it is possible to create molds of wooden, stone, chalk, etc., objects. From these molds, even the slightest details may be reproduced, which can then be "printed" on raw material.

To make a mould, soften the material a little. The polymer must be able to assume the shape of the object on which it is pressed and to reproduce its slightest details.

To detach it from the original model, it is necessary to use an external agent, such as baby powder. Should you want to reproduce the relief of an object, for example a cameo or a motif in wood, put the whole

MATERIAL REQUIRED

VASE, WHITE RESIN (20 GR.), RED RESIN (40 GR.).
A MOULD WITH A FLOWER MOTIF, SCISSORS,
ROLLING PIN, PAINTBRUSH, BABY POWDER, CUTTER,
EQUIPMENT NECESSARY FOR BAKING

lot in the oven, after having sprinkled the surface to be copied with baby powder and covered it completely with some paste. In this way, when the heat of the oven softens the resin, you do not risk your creation being deformed. On the contrary, even the smallest details will be reproduced.

Some polymers, after baking, are more flexible than others and it is therefore advisable to use the former to make molds. We shall use a flower motif as an example. Naturally you yourselves can create other motifs to reproduce.

FLOWER VASES

In this project we have used the actual flowers to decorate the rim of a flower vase. This vase can be put out of doors because the paste does not undergo alteration, whether from rain or sun shine. The mould with the flower motif was made by distributing small balls on a plane of resin. One of these balls was put in the middle and the remaining six arranged all around. With a toothpick, holes were made on the central part and rays traced round this part so as to create small decorative channels on the petals.

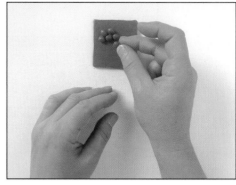

MAKING THE MOULD

Spread a sheet of resin and make six small balls. Apply one of them to the paste, as the center of the flower. Distribute the remaining ones around, as if they were petals.

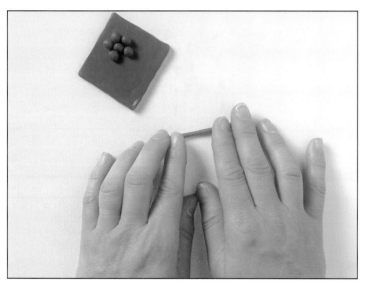

Roll a small quantity of resin, enough to make a cord, and attach it as the flower stem. Complete the flower with the leaves, placing them at the sides of the stem.

With a toothpick, make a series of holes in the middle part of the flower. Around the center, on the petals, make some lines similar to the sun's rays.
Once completed, put in the oven and bake for 20 minutes at 130°C.

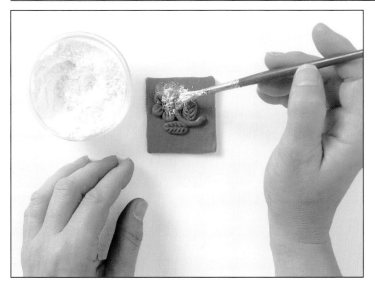

Leave to cool. Then, with a brush, sprinkle the surface with baby powder so that every dot is covered in white. With some paste make a round shape. Squeeze it onto the mould until every space is covered.

Put the whole lot, the baked mould and the shape still to bake, into the oven for 20 minutes at 130°C. Leave to cool. Remove the mould. You will see that every single detail has been reproduced.

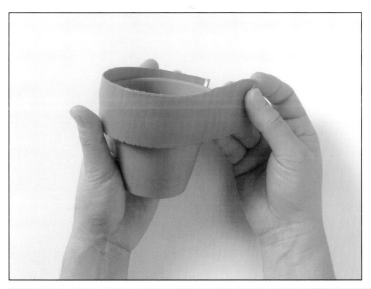

USING THE MOULD

Cut a strip of resin as long as the vase rim and a little wider than its frame.
Press on to the rim and be sure it adheres well.

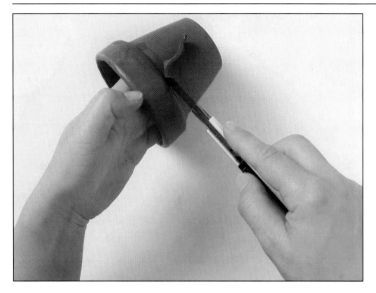

With a cutter, remove any excess paste. Eliminate from the inside rim any excess paste while still leaving dome tucked in.

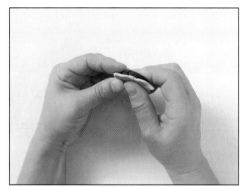

Sprinkle the mould with baby powder with the help of a paintbrush. Press some white resin into the mould.

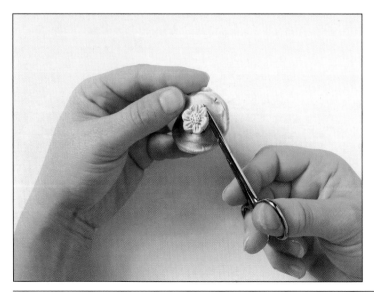

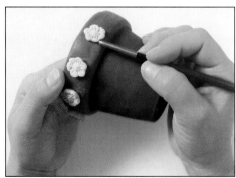

Detach the resin and cut the outline of the shape with a pair of scissors. Create in this way seven flowers to apply around the vase. Apply the motif on the rim covered in resin and, with the top part of the paintbrush, make the paste adhere to the surface.

YELLOW FRAME

The frame used in this project can hold either a mirror or a photograph. The mould of the frame was derived from the edge of a carved, wooden box. You could reproduce motifs from old frames so as to have an "L" shaped mould.
The "L" shape was chosen because it can be applied both on the long and short sides of the frame. It also gives you the possibility of choosing the place in which the motif must be interrupted to join on to the next section.
The drawing must have a certain continuity, but with

MATERIAL REQUIRED

A WOODEN FRAME 10 X 13 CM, GOLD RESIN (80 GR.),
AN "L" SHAPED MOULD, BABY POWDER, ROLLING PIN,
PAINTBRUSH AND CUTTER,
EQUIPMENT NECESSARY FOR BAKING

a little skill, you can 'hide' certain inconsistencies which could arise from joining two sections together. This project requires particular attention when applying the resin.
The paste must adhere well to the wooden support and must be manipulated for a long time. This is why I advise you complete the frame in two stages:
- Cover the frame with a thin sheet of paste.
- Apply the mould of the motif chosen for the frame on a previously worked base.

Make a thin sheet of gold resin, cut into four trapezoids and apply to the frame. Tuck in all the edges well.

Finish off the channels and joionings with the tip of a paintbrush. With some soft resin, prepare a sheet with the shape of an "L". The material used to reproduce the motif must be thin.

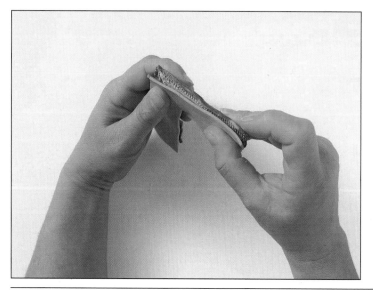

Apply the sheet of paste over the mould and press the whole surface for a while so that the resin covers the whole mould well. Place the mould on the frame covered in resin.

With a cutter, cut away the protruding edges. Finish off and attach the motif, helping yourselves with the tip of the paintbrush handle.

Making sure not to squash the previous applications, complete the decoration of the frame and cut away any excess resin. Again, use the tip of the brush handle to give the finishing touches to the joining point of the motif.

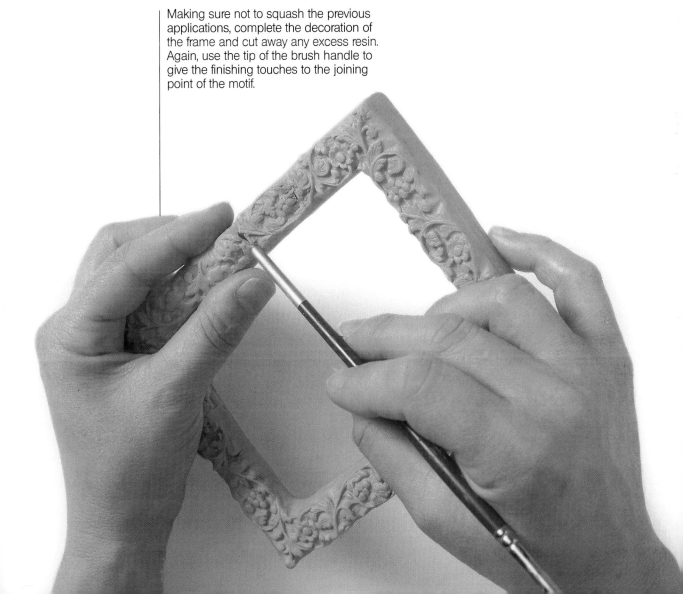

INLAID ENGRAVINGS

CUTTING TECHNIQUE
Our plastic material can be cut and engraved. In the two following projects, we shall use molds for making small cakes, which can usually be found in shops selling kitchenware.
The shapes are engraved on a thin surface. The sectioned part of the material is removed and you can choose whether to leave the delimited motif "empty" or to replace it with another sheet of a different colored resin, inlay style.

MATERIAL REQUIRED

SMALL MOLDS, SMALL AMOUNTS OF RED, PINK, YELLOW AND WHITE "TRANSPARENT" RESIN, LIGHT BLUE RESIN (20 GR.), GREEN RESIN (65 GR.), SCISSORS, PENCIL, ERASER, A PIECE OF GLASS AS BIG AS THE SHAPE OF AN LAMP, CUTTER, BI-ADHESIVE TAPE, METAL STRUCTURE FOR THE ABAT-JOUR, EQUIPMENT NECESSARY FOR BAKING

The first project will fill in the empty spaces, while the second one concentrates on making a candleholder with material-free areas.

LAMP
Constructing a lamp is not difficult, but it requires a lot of patience and attention. To prevent your work from damage, you must bake it in various stages. In other words, we must give "stability" to the first phase before passing on to the second one.
Two bakings are sufficient to complete the projects.

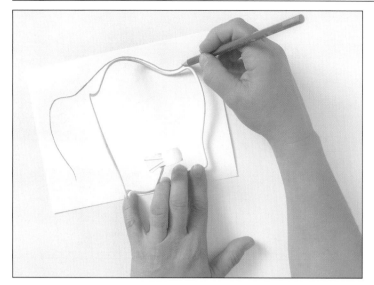

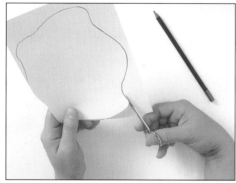

With a pencil, draw the outline of the structure on a sheet of paper. Cut the shape with a pair of scissors. It will serve as a stencil to determine the outline of the lamp on the resin.

On a piece of glass spread a thin layer of green plastic material so that it covers 4/5 of the height of the lamp. Make a rectangle and attach on it a strip of light blue resin. The resulting rectangle must be big enough to fit the outline of the lamp. Make sure that the two colors are well joined at all points.

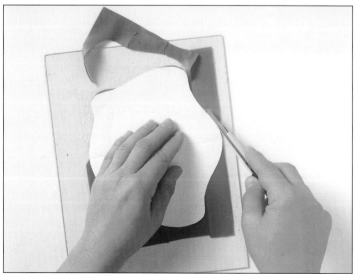

Place the stencil on the rectangle and cut the contour of the shape. Take some molds and engrave the resin, so as to obtain a regular decoration with these figures. Remove the material engraved.

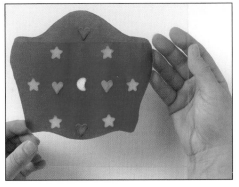

With pink, red, yellow and white paste make the shapes necessary to fill in the empty spaces and fit them in. Without removing your work from the piece of glass, put in a cool oven and bake at 130°C for 15 minutes. Leave to cool in the oven.

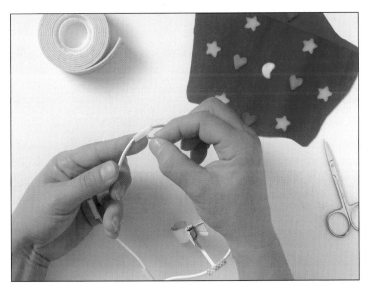

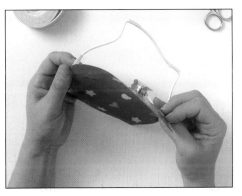

Cut small pieces of bi-adhesive cello tape and place on the back of the metal structure. Once you have coated the edges of the shape, the cello tape can be removed. Detach the resin from the glass and arrange it on the metal structure, making sure to position it properly.

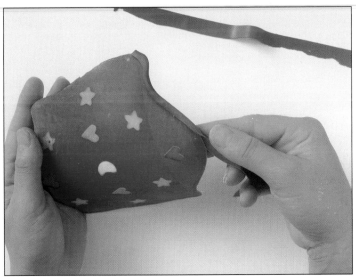

Prepare a long, thin strip of light blue resin to apply around the shape, both as support and as a finishing touch. Remove the pieces of adhesive tape as you advance with the strip of resin. At this stage, the object must be baked once more. It is important that the object be out in the oven with the lamina facing upwards, otherwise, due to its weight, it could detach itself from the border during baking. Furthermore, if the lamina doesn't rest on a surface while in the oven, it tends to sink. This can be solved by placing a curved piece of cardboard to act as a support or by removing the object from the oven while it is still relatively hot, manually restoring its initial shape.

INLAY

CANDLEHOLDER
Coating glass containers is one of the possible applications of synthetic paste.
The project we propose in these pages is a candleholder, with the aim of exploiting the characteristics of transparency that can be obtained by reducing the material to a very thin sheet.
Furthermore, the inlay technique makes it possible to create shapes which are then highlighted when illuminated from within. For this project you will need a pasta machine in order to obtain a thin sheet of resin.
Given the fact that the work must be carried out in various sections, you can happily use a rolling pin, making sure, however, to roll the material as much as possible.

MATERIAL REQUIRED

A COGNAC GLASS, MOLDS USED FOR MAKING SMALL CAKES, LIGHT BLUE RESIN (40 GR.), ROLLING PIN, CUTTER. EQUIPMENT NECESSARY FOR BAKING

Make thin sheets of resin and apply on to the glass until the glass is completely covered. If the sheet of resin is thin enough, you need only press slightly for it to adhere well to the glass.

Once the glass has been covered completely, engrave some shapes using molds which can be bought in shops selling kitchenware. Remove the engraved resin, so that the glass is visible. Bake in the oven at 130°C for 15 minutes.

MOSAIC

Mosaics go back a long time: already in ancient Mesopotamia, in 3000 BC, mosaics were used to pave the streets with stones of different colors. In ancient Rome, walls, ceilings and floors in both public and private places were decorated with mosaics. These decorations are made with small tessera in glass or other materials and glued on to a support. A small space is left between one tessera and the other, which is later filled with sealing cement.

The glass normally used to make mosaics is not transparent. It has nonetheless a glossy surface. With resin it is possible to obtain the glass effect typical of mosaics. The advantage in using synthetic paste is that it can be cut easily with a cutter or a pair of scissors. The pieces thus obtained can be worked with the technique used for traditional mosaic or can

> **MATERIAL REQUIRED**
>
> A BOTTLE, A SHEET OF GLASS, CUTTER (OR SCISSORS), YELLOW RESIN (5 GR.), PINK (5 GR), LIGHT BLUE (20 GR) AND GREY (25 GR.) EQUIPMENT NECESSARY FOR BAKING

be applied, as in our project, on a soft layer of polymer. For the surface to achieve the glossy look, use a piece of glass as a base for baking.
The area in contact with the piece of glass will remain glossy even after baking. Should you wish to have a wide variety of tesserae you can, besides making them in different colors, cover some with gold laminae, purpurin or shiny powders.
The mosaic technique is simple: it is a meticulous job, but can give great satisfaction. If you have a rich imagination, you can create pictures, line frames etc as if you were really using the mosaic technique.
For the vase, we shall use the polymer itself as sealing agent. We shall first make the tesserae which, once baked, will be placed in soft resin, to which they will be "attached" during the second baking.

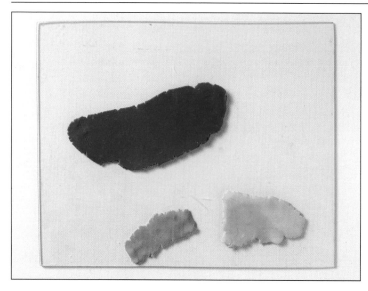

Roll some pink, yellow and light blue on a glass surface. Put in the oven and bake for 15 minutes at 130°C. Leave to cool. Cut the laminae with a pair of scissors or a cutter into many tesserae.

Cover the bottle with some very soft, grey material. It is important that the resin should have been kneaded at a previous stage.

Complete the borders and start to apply the pieces of polymer, leaving some space between them. Exercise the right amount of pressure on each tessera so that it adheres well to the still unbaked resin.

Continue until the whole surface is covered. Check that the tesserae are well placed in the resin: grey resin must be visible all round. Put the object in the oven and bake for 30 minutes at 130°C. Leave to cool.

MOKUMÉ GANE

Mokumé Gane is an old technique for working metals originating in Japan. Various layers of different colored metals are overlaid and given an undulating shape, creating protruding parts. The humps are eliminated so that the underlying colored layers become visible. The

MATERIAL REQUIRED

RESIN OF FOUR VIVID COLORS, ROLLING PIN, CUTTER, PIECE OF CARDBOARD, A PEN TO WRITE THE GUESTS' NAMES AND A TOOTHPICK. EQUIPMENT NECESSARY FOR BAKING

different streaks create very decorative, abstract motifs.

PLACE MARKS
This project is very simple to make, and can be made a couple of hours before your guests arrive. They will certainly give a very original touch to your table.

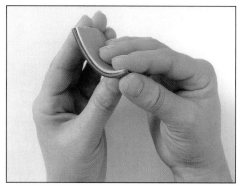

Roll four thin layers of resin 6 x 3 cm. Decide which of the colors you would rather have on the outside and superimpose the laminae one over the other. Squeeze one of the shortest sides of this four-layered plane.

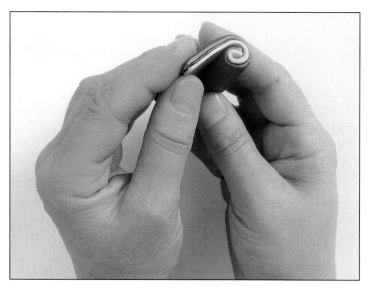

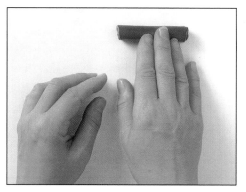

Roll, beginning from the thinned down side. Make sure that the color you have chosen to remain on the outside is indeed on the outside. Roll the log until it measures 19 cm (with about 1 cm diameter).

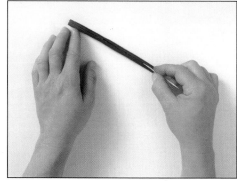

With the aid of a sharp paring knife, now cut about 5 cm down the middle of this strip of resin. To the right and left of this cut mark a shallow canal with a toothpick.

Prepare a piece of cardboard, about 4 cm wide and 8 cm high. Insert it in the cut until you have covered 1/2 of its length. Fold the "sausage" so that the edges of the piece of card fit into the canals marked.

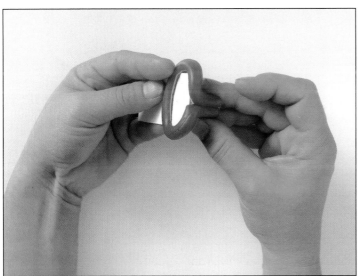

Wrap the card until the two extremities touch in the center of the lower part. Join them together so as to create a pedestal for the place mark. Start decorating with the Mokumé Gane technique.

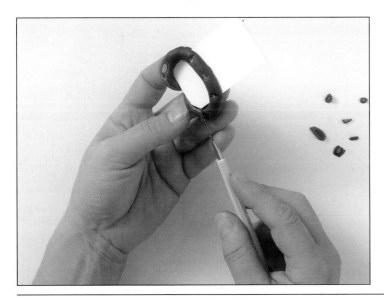

Cut small superficial slices which will render the various layers visible.
During baking, the resin tends to soften and the object, under its weight, could end up deformed.
To prevent this from happening, place a toothpick between the card and the pedestal. Put the whole lot (card, toothpick and resin) in the oven for 20 minutes at 130°C.

INLAYS

The inlay technique has its origins in the East. The first marble inlays were discovered in Asia Minor, at Alicarnasse in 350 BC. This technique is usually carried out on wood, but it can also be made with ivory, mother-of-pearl, precious stones and other materials. The image or decoration is made with small pieces of wood or other types of material. The inlay technique with wood or stones requires a lot of precision because every single piece

> MATERIAL REQUIRED
>
> WHITE, ORANGE, YELLOW, RED AND LIGHT BLUE "TRANSPARENT" TYPE RESIN (THE AMOUNTS ARE NOT INDICATED BECAUSE THEY DON'T EXCEED 10 GR.), TRACING PAPER, PENCIL, TOOTHPICK, CUTTER, ROLLING PIN, SHEET OF GLASS (10 CM X 15 CM), EQUIPMENT NECESSARY FOR BAKING

must fit perfectly with the adjacent one. When using synthetic pastes there is no risk of making mistakes.

"VITREAUX"
In this project we shall use polymers which give our work a relatively transparent effect. The inlay technique will be applied but, thanks to the properties of the resin, the motif created can be used as a decoration to be hung on a window.

With a pencil and a sheet of tracing paper, copy the picture: a flower, with a two-colored center, orange petals and a green stem. Pressing slightly, pass a toothpick over the outline of the petals so as to leave a mark on the paste.

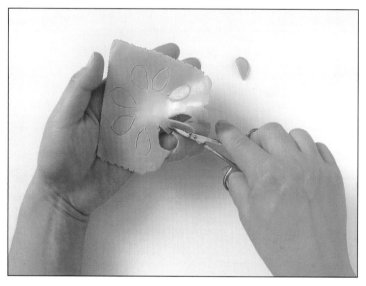

With a pair of scissors, cut the petals engraved on the orange resin. Place a sheet of glass on the picture and then, on top of this, start arranging the petals in correspondence with the picture.

With regard the central part, roll very little red resin and proceed as with the petals. Place the already cut center over this, thus reproducing the original drawing. Arrange the stem and the leaves.

Once you have cut the leaves, following the same steps as those for the petals and the center of the flower, place them as depicted in the drawing under the sheet of glass. The first step of the work is now completed. Put in the oven for 15 minutes at 130°C and leave to cool.

The first half of the inlay, once baked, will not amalgamate with the material added at a later stage. The final work will be perfectly delimited in every part, th outline and cut. Certain operations may turn out incomplete due to tiny defects during working. If so, just add very small portions of material and model the area on the same frame.

Prendete del colore giallo ed inseritelo nel centro, in modo che sia tutt'uno con a parte adiacente. Per verificare se ogni punto è unito, sarà sufficiente alzare il vetro e controllare la situazione controluce.
Per inserire il campo dell'immagine, seguirete gli stessi passi fatti per tutti gli elementi della figura: stendete la pasta, delimitate i contorni e tagliate.
Certe rientranze rimangono facilmente incompiute, a causa di piccole imprecisioni durante la lavorazione.
In tal caso, basterà aggiungere minute porzioni di materiale e modellare l'area sulla stessa formella.

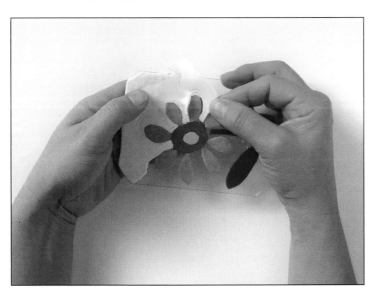

If the background is too difficult to handle, apply it in various stages.
Use a toothpick to help you unite the interrupted areas. Once the drawing appears perfect on its surface, put in the oven and bake for 15 minutes at 130°C.

MODELLING SMALL SHAPES

CHRISTMAS TREE UNDER THE SNOW

Having been born and bred in hot places, where snow exists only in fables, I have always appreciated those magic balls with cities covered in snow inside. Should you one day decide to spend Christmas in the southern hemisphere, take with you the tree proposed in the following pages because there the snow is nothing but a dream.

Most objects can be made with basic forms: balls, logs, sheets, cones, cubes, etc. Our Christmas corner is made with these simple structures.

> **MATERIAL REQUIRED**
>
> A SMALL GLASS (THOSE USED FOR COFFEE), WATER, CUTTER, SCISSORS, SILICONE, PURPURIN, NAFTALI. RESINS OF THE FOLLOWING COLORS: WHITE (10 GR.), GREEN (10 GR.), LIGHT GREEN (20 GR.), PINK (5 GR.), RED (15 GR.), PURPLE (5 GR.), YELLOW (5 GR.), BLUE (5 GR.) AND BROWN (5 GR.) BESIDE EQUIPMENT NECESSARY FOR BAKING

You must check that the dimensions of the work are right, otherwise they will not fit into the glass.

CHRISTMAS CRIB

To make the characters of the crib, basic shapes were used, such as cones for the body, spheres for the head, and sheets of paste for the cloaks. The faces are just slices of murrhines with the face motif applied to a ball of material. By reducing the murrhine, you will obtain faces of different sizes, so you can have a small face for Jesus. Instead of using a glass, the top section of a plastic bottle was used.

With a cutter, cut a small brown cylinder to make the vase to house the pine tree. Stick a toothpick inside the cylinder to act as the tree's support.

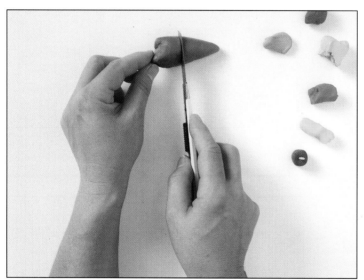

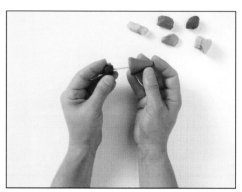

With a cone made of dark green resin, make the tree. Insert the toothpick into the cone.

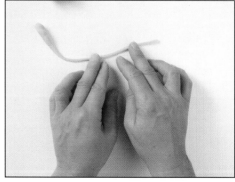

Make a small cube with some red resin, which will be one of the Christmas parcels. After having made other cubes with blue, pink and purple resin, create a very thin string with yellow resin.

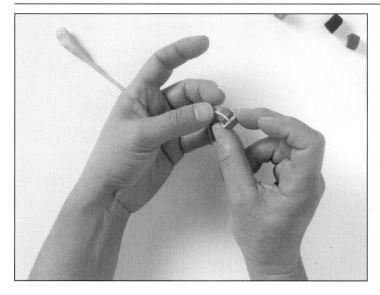

Tie the yellow string bow-like around the presents, which will be arranged around the tree. Use a toothpick to help you with the knot.

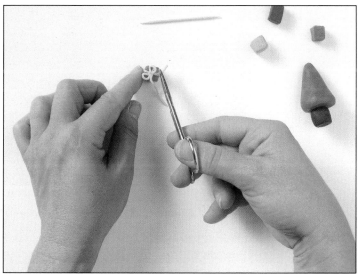

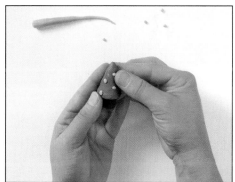

Cut the string with a pair of scissors. Apply small decorative balls into the tree and press slightly for them to adhere well.

Soften the green polymer and make a ball by rolling the material between the palms of your hands. Flatten the ball until it assumes the shape of a disk, with which cover the mouth of the glass vase.

Press a glass on the green disk. Decorate the tree with purpurin.

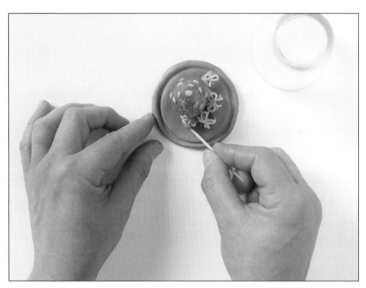

Arrange the composition on the green disk and make sure all the pieces adhere well to the base because, once completed, they will be immersed in water. With the toothpick, mark the base, create the effect of grass.

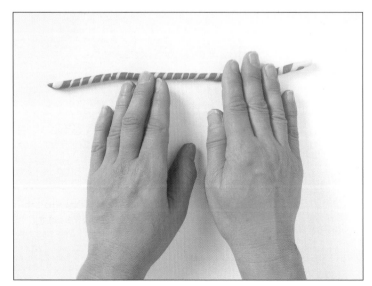

Roll two strings of red and white resin together. Elongate the resulting string until it is long enough to outline the whole base. Apply it all around as a decoration.

Sprinkle the rim of the glass with baby powder. Turn upside down onto the surface. Put the tree in a cool oven. Bring the temperature to 130°C and bake for 20 minutes.

Fill the glass with water, leaving some space for the object. Grate some mothballs and pour into the water.

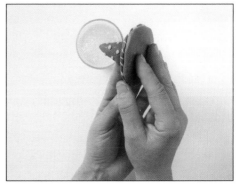

With some silicone, fill the canal around the composition. Close the glass containing your work. The rim of the glass must fit nicely into the canal. Leave the glue to dry before turning your work over.

INDEX